Collins

Maths

Year 4 Maths
Targeted Practice Workbook

Age
8 – 9

Year 4

Targeted
Practice
Workbook

$$12 \times 6 =$$
$$672 + 281 =$$
$$91 - 38 =$$
$$54 \div 6 =$$

Tom Hall

Contents

Contents

PS **50.** This graph shows the number of lengths some friends swam.
Altogether they swam 25 lengths.

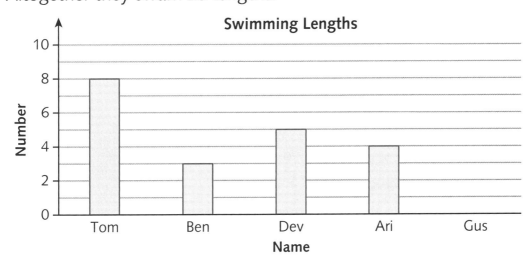

a) Who swan 3 lengths? _____

b) How many more lengths did Tom swim
than Dev? _____ lengths

c) How many lengths did Gus swim? _____ lengths

d) Complete the bar chart with the bar for Gus.

4 marks

PS **51.** This pictogram shows the number of dogs that live in four streets.

	🐕 represents 2 dogs
Street	**Number of dogs**
Oak Street	🐕 🐕 🐕 🐕
Ivy Street	🐕 🐕 🐕
Elm Street	🐕 🐕 🐕 🐕 🐕
Ash Street	🐕 🐕 🐕 🐕

a) How many dogs live in Ash Street? _____ dogs

b) How many more dogs live in Elm Street than
in Ivy Street? _____ dogs

c) A new street is added. 12 dogs live in Birch Street.

How many dog symbols will show 12 dogs? _____ symbols

3 marks

Counting

PS〉 Problem-solving questions

Challenge 1

1 Fill in the missing terms in these sequences.

   a) 0   8   16   24   32   _____   _____

   b) 18   24   30   36   42   _____   _____

   2 marks

2 What is the rule for each sequence of numbers?

   a) (6 12 18 24 30 😊)   _____

   b) (250 275 300 325 350 😊)   _____

   2 marks

PS **3** Nia is counting in sevens. Will 80 be in Nia's sequence? _____

   1 mark

PS **4** Poppy counts in sixes.

   | 36 | 42 | 48 | 56 | 60 |

   Which number is incorrect?   _____

   1 mark

Marks.......... /6

Challenge 2

1 Fill in the missing terms in these sequences.

   a) 18   24   30   36   _____   _____

   b) 150   175   _____   _____   250   275

   2 marks

2 What is the rule for each sequence of numbers?

   a) 70   77   84   91   98   _____

   b) 400   425   450   475   500   _____

   2 marks

Counting

PS **3** This number grid is damaged.

What number would be in the last square?

_____

275	300	325	350
375	400	425	
475			
575			

1 mark

Marks.......... /5

Challenge 3

1 Fill in the next three terms in this sequence.

 99 108 117 126

1 mark

2 The numbers in this sequence add the same number.
Fill in the missing terms.

54				78

1 mark

PS **3** Polly is counting in nines: 45   54   63   71   81   90

Which number is incorrect?   _____

1 mark

4 Here is a number grid.
Moving right the numbers add 7.
Moving down the numbers add 9.
Fill in the missing numbers.

Add 7 ⟶

Add 9 ↓

21	28	35	42	49
30	37	44		58
39		53	60	67
48	55	62	69	76

1 mark

Marks.......... /4

Total marks .... /15

How am I doing?

Numbers Beyond 1000

PS Problem-solving questions

Challenge 1

1 Write < or > in each circle to make these statements correct.

a) 4308 ◯ 4380   b) 3681 ◯ 3618   c) 5283 ◯ 5286

3 marks

2 Tick the correct statement.

A 3670 < 3669 ☐   B 5410 < 3409 ☐   C 1872 < 2890 ☐

1 mark

3 Write these numbers in order, starting with the smallest.

3563   4645   4536   4654   3465

_____   _____   _____   _____   _____

1 mark

PS **4** Gary has these four digit cards.

5   7   4   1

What is the largest four-digit number Gary can make? _____

1 mark

Marks.......... /6

Challenge 2

1 Write < or > in each circle to make these statements correct.

a) 5437 ◯ 4437   b) 2718 ◯ 2721   c) 4324 ◯ 4342

3 marks

2 Write these numbers in order, starting with the smallest.

4831   4138   5642   5246   5264

_____   _____   _____   _____   _____

1 mark

Numbers Beyond 1000

PS **3** Tao has these five digit cards.

6   3   8   5   1

a) What is the largest three-digit number Tao can make? _____

b) What is the smallest four-digit number Tao can make? _____

2 marks

Marks.......... /6

Challenge 3

1 Write these numbers in order, starting with the smallest.

681   **7861**   **12 612**   **5891**   **11 937**

_____   _____   _____   _____   _____

1 mark

PS **2** Manisha writes four numbers in order, starting with the smallest.

6278   6285   ?   6290

What could the missing number be? _____

1 mark

PS **3** The number of people at five football matches is recorded.

Match	Number of people
Rovers vs Town	12 834
City vs Rangers	9452
United vs Albion	10 099
County vs North End	13 901
Athletic vs Wanderers	9078

Which match had the smallest number of people?

_____

1 mark

Marks.......... /3

Total marks .... /15   How am I doing?

Place Value

PS Problem-solving questions

Challenge 1

1 What is the value of the 4 in each of these numbers?

a) 3549 _____ b) 7427 _____ c) 8194 _____

 3 marks

2 Circle the number that has a digit with a value of 7 tens.

5752   8967   1475

1 mark

3 Circle the number that has a digit with a value of 3 hundreds.

36   341   4103

 1 mark

PS **4** Arrange these numbers to make a four-digit number. _____

7 ones   6 hundreds   2 tens   3 thousands

1 mark

Marks.......... /6

Challenge 2

1 What is the value of the 9 in each of these numbers?

a) 7920 _____ b) 6295 _____ c) 9302 _____

3 marks

2 Circle the number that has a digit with a value of 8 hundreds.

 8006   3890   1080

1 mark

3 Write the total of 8 + 700 + 30 + 9000. _____

1 mark

4 Write the total of 4 tens + 3 hundreds +
2 ones + 6 thousands. _____

1 mark

Place Value

PS **5** Here are five digit cards.

| 4 | 3 | 5 | 6 | 2 |

a) Use any four cards to make a number larger than 5000. _____

b) Use any four cards to make the smallest four-digit number possible. _____

2 marks

Marks.........../8

Challenge 3

PS **1** Jamie says, "4021 is smaller than 897 because it has smaller numbers."

Explain to Jamie why he is incorrect.

_____

_____

1 mark

PS **2** Nisha is thinking of a four-digit number.
Use the clues below to work out Nisha's number. _____

- When you add the four digits, the total is 10.
- The thousands digit is 6.
- The tens digit is half the thousands digit.
- The ones digit is 1.

1 mark

3 Work out the number that is:

a) one ten more than 9999. _____

b) one hundred more than 9990.

2 marks

Marks.........../4

Total marks ..../18   How am I doing?   😊 😐 😖

Roman Numerals

PS Problem-solving questions

Challenge 1

1 Change these Roman numerals to numbers.

a) XII _____   b) XV _____   c) XXVI _____

d) VIII _____   e) XXXIII _____   f) XL _____

6 marks

2 Here are some Roman calculations. Write them using numbers.

a) III + II = V   b) VI + IV = X

_____ + _____ = _____   _____ + _____ = _____

c) XXVI – VII = XIX

_____ – _____ = _____

3 marks

PS **3** Write the time shown on each clock.

a)

b)

_____   _____

2 marks

Marks.......... /11

Challenge 2

1 Change these Roman numerals to numbers.

a) LVI = _____   b) XLVIII = _____

c) XCVI = _____   d) LXXXIII = _____

4 marks

2 Write the next Roman numeral in the sequence as a number.

LXXXVI   LXXXVII   LXXXVIII   LXXXIX   _____

1 mark

Roman Numerals

3 Here are some Roman calculations. Write them using numbers.

a) XL + LX = C

_____ + _____ = _____

b) LXIX – XXX = XXXIX

_____ – _____ = _____

2 marks

4 Circle the Roman numeral that is equivalent to 99.

 IC   CX   XCXI   XCIX   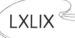 LXLIX

1 mark

Marks.........../8

Challenge 3

1 Write these Roman numerals in order of size, smallest first.

XC   **LXV**   **XXXVIII**   **LXIX**   **XLVII**

smallest | | | | | largest

1 mark

2 Complete these calculations. Write your answers as numbers.

a) LXIV – XLVII + XXIX = _____

b) XXIV + XIX + XCIII = _____

c) XL + LX – L = _____

d) XXXIX – XXI + LXVI = _____

4 marks

3 These Roman numerals are larger than 100. Write them as numbers.

a) CXXV _____   **b)** CCXXII _____

c) CCCLIX _____

3 marks

Marks.........../8

Total marks ..../27   How am I doing?

19

Representing Numbers

PS Problem-solving questions

Challenge 1

1 Estimate the numbers the arrows point to.

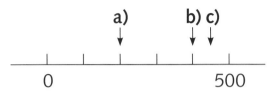

a) _____

b) _____

c) _____

3 marks

2 Write the number shown on each abacus.

a)

b)

_____   _____

2 marks

3 Write these numbers using digits.

a) Five thousand, two hundred and ninety-six = _____

b) Seven thousand, five hundred and seventy = _____

c) Two thousand, eight hundred and four = _____

3 marks

Marks.......... /8

Challenge 2

1 Write the three-digit number represented by these blocks. _____

1 mark

2 Look at this calculation: $2538 = 2000 + 500 + 30 + 8$

Write these numbers in a similar way.

a) $4825 = $ _____ + _____ + _____ + _____

b) $6719 = $ _____ + _____ + _____ + _____

2 marks

Representing Numbers

3 Estimate the numbers the arrows point to.

a) _____

b) _____

c) _____

3 marks

Marks.......... /6

Challenge 3

PS **1** 6538 can be written as 6000 + 400 + 130 + 8.

Find five ways to write 3746.

a) _____   b) _____

c) _____   d) _____

e) _____

5 marks

2 Write these numbers as digits.

a) Four thousand, six hundred and nine   _____

b) Eight thousand and twenty   _____

2 marks

3 Complete the following.

a) 7000 = _____ thousands = _____ hundreds

= _____ tens = _____ ones

b) 80 tens = _____   c) 30 hundreds = _____

3 marks

4 Use these place value cards to write a four-digit number. _____

| 7 hundreds | 8 ones | 2 thousands | 3 tens |

1 mark

Marks.......... /11

Total marks .... /25   How am I doing?

21

Rounding Numbers

PS Problem-solving questions

Challenge 1

1 Round each number to the nearest 10.

a) 54 _____   b) 99 _____   c) 76 _____

3 marks

2 Enrico is rounding numbers to the nearest 10.
Circle the numbers he will round to 80.

72   84   75   85   77

3 marks

PS **3** Jo estimates the answer to 52 + 74 by rounding both numbers to the nearest 10 and adding.

Write Jo's estimated answer. _____

1 mark

4 Round each number to the nearest 100.

a) 326 _____   b) 704 _____   c) 1477 _____

3 marks

Marks......... /10

Challenge 2

1 Round each number to the nearest 100.

a) 3783 _____   b) 6317 _____   c) 5078 _____

3 marks

2 Round 2628 to the:

a) nearest 10. _____

b) nearest 100. _____

c) nearest 1000. _____

3 marks

3 Round each number to the nearest 1000.

a) 4009 _____   b) 2505 _____   c) 8199 _____

3 marks

Rounding Numbers

4 Sean rounded a number to the nearest 100. His answer was 700.

Write three different numbers that Sean's number could have been.

_____   _____   _____

3 marks

Marks.........../12

Challenge 3

1 Round each number to the nearest 1000.

a) 6043 _____   b) 789 _____   c) 3911 _____

3 marks

PS **2** Max has a secret number.
He rounds the number down to the nearest 1000, the answer is 7000.
He rounds the same number to the nearest 10, the answer is 7340.

Write a possible secret number.   _____

1 mark

3 Oliver rounds numbers to the nearest 10.
Circle the numbers Oliver has rounded.

350   4005   6000   7900   10 101

3 marks

4 Eve has four numbers cards.
She makes four-digit numbers using the cards and rounds them to the nearest 1000.

5   9   6   1

Write the 4 four-digit numbers that Eve will round to 7000.

_____   _____   _____   _____

4 marks

Marks.........../11

Total marks ..../33   How am I doing?

23

Negative Numbers

Challenge 1

$$-6 \quad -5 \quad -4 \quad -3 \quad -2 \quad -1 \quad 0 \quad 1 \quad 2 \quad 3 \quad 4 \quad 5 \quad 6$$

1 Use the number line.

a) Start at 3, count back 5, write the number you reach. _____

b) Start at 2, count back 6, write the number you reach. _____

c) Start at 5, count back 7, write the number you reach. _____

d) Start at 4, count back 9, write the number you reach. _____

4 marks

2 Calculate by counting backwards:

a) $4 - 6 =$ _____   b) $3 - 7 =$ _____   c) $5 - 6 =$ _____

3 marks

PS **3** Jake wants to buy a t-shirt for £7. He has £3.
He borrows the rest from his dad.
How much does Jake owe his dad? _____

1 mark

4 Start at –2, count back 3, write the number you reach. _____

1 mark

Marks.......... /9

Challenge 2

1 a) Start at 4, count back 8, write the number you reach. _____

b) Start at 2, count back 9, write the number you reach. _____

c) Start at 10, count back 12, write the number you reach. _____

d) Start at 1, count back 10, write the number you reach. _____

4 marks

2 Calculate by counting backwards:

a) $2 - 7 =$ _____   b) $12 - 17 =$ _____   c) $15 - 16 =$ _____

3 marks

3 Calculate by counting backwards:

a) $-2 - 7 =$ _____   b) $-5 - 12 =$ _____   c) $-10 - 8 =$ _____

3 marks

Negative Numbers

PS **4** Look at the thermometer.

Write the temperature after these changes.

a) The temperature is 12°C and falls by 14°C. _____

b) The temperature is –4°C and falls by 5°C. _____

c) The temperature is –3°C and rises by 7°C. _____

3 marks

Marks......... /13

Challenge 3

1 Arrange these numbers in order, starting with the largest.

$$-6 \quad 5 \quad -1 \quad -4 \quad 3$$

largest ☐☐☐☐☐ smallest

1 mark

2 This number line runs from –10 to 10. Four arrows point to whole numbers. Write the numbers the arrows point to.

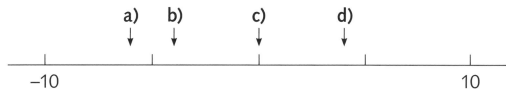

a) _____ b) _____ c) _____ d) _____

4 marks

3 Calculate:

a) $3 - 12 = $ _____ b) $5 - 20 = $ _____ c) $12 - 20 = $ _____

d) $-5 - 9 = $ _____ e) $-12 - 12 = $ _____ f) $-8 + 4 = $ _____

6 marks

Marks.......... /11

Total marks .... /33   How am I doing?

25

Addition and Subtraction Practice

1 Work out the answers to these addition problems.

a)
```
   3 2 7
 + 4 2 2
 _____
```

b)
```
   7 9 2
 + 2 0 5
 _____
```

c)
```
   4 9 2
 + 5 1 3
 _____
```

3 marks

2 Work out the answers to these subtraction problems.

a)
```
   6 5 8
 − 2 5 7
 _____
```

b)
```
   5 8 8
 − 4 9 7
 _____
```

c)
```
   7 0 1
 − 1 7 3
 _____
```

3 marks

Marks.......... /6

1 Work out the answers to these addition problems.

a)
```
   8 5 4
 + 6 7 4
 _____
```

b)
```
   8 3 9
 + 5 7 9
 _____
```

c)
```
   8 8 4 4
 + 4 8 8 4
 _____
```

3 marks

Addition and Subtraction Practice

2 Work out the answers to these subtraction problems.

a)
```
    9  0  3
 -  2  6  0
 _____
```

b)
```
    7  9  0
 -  3  8  4
 _____
```

c)
```
    5  3  3  1
 -  1  7  3  5
 _____
```

3 marks

Marks.......... /6

Challenge 3

1 Work out the answers to these addition problems.

a)
```
    5  9  2  1
 +  6  4  7  9
 _____
```

b)
```
    8  5  3  6
 +  2  7  7  6
 _____
```

c)
```
    6  4  3  7
 +  6  4  7  2
 _____
```

3 marks

2 Work out the answers to these subtraction problems.

a)
```
    6  6  7  3
 -  5  4  7  7
 _____
```

b)
```
    9  0  6  3
 -  5  0  9  0
 _____
```

c)
```
    8  4  7  2
 -  3  6  7  9
 _____
```

3 marks

Marks.......... /6

Total marks .... /18   How am I doing?

Estimating and Checking Calculations

Challenge 1

1 Round each number to the nearest 10. Then use the rounded numbers to give an estimated answer to each calculation.

a) 54 + 74 _____

b) 33 + 64 _____

c) 76 + 85 _____

3 marks

PS **2** Tara calculates 125 + 265 = 390. She wants to check her calculation by calculating the inverse.

Circle the calculation that is the inverse of Tara's calculation.

| 265 + 390 | 390 – 265 | 390 + 125 | 265 – 125 |

1 mark

3 Write the inverse of each calculation.

a) 235 + 328 = 563 b) 529 – 236 = 293 c) 525 – 214 = 311

_____ _____ _____

3 marks

PS **4** A gardener plants tulip and daffodil bulbs. Altogether, there are 486 bulbs. She plants 259 tulip bulbs.

How many are daffodil bulbs? _____

1 mark

Marks.......... /8

Challenge 2

PS **1** Joshua thinks of a number. He adds 56 to the number. Joshua's answer is 412.

What was Joshua's number? _____

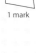

1 mark

PS **2** Kia thinks of a number. She subtracts 94 from the number. Kia's answer is 536.

What was Kia's number? _____

1 mark

Estimating and Checking Calculations

3 Estimate the answers to these calculations by rounding to the nearest 100.

a) 418 + 629 _____

b) 907 – 798 _____

2 marks

4 Estimate the answers to these calculations by rounding to the nearest 1000.

a) 6321 – 2976 _____

b) 6602 + 3532 _____

2 marks

Marks.......... /6

Challenge 3

PS **1** Bryn estimates the price of two pens as 50p and 80p by rounding to the nearest 10p. The actual cost of the two pens is £1.35.

What could the price of each pen have been? _____ and _____

1 mark

PS **2** Estimate answers to these calculations by rounding to the nearest 1000.

a) 7286 + 9781 _____

b) 12 084 – 6822 _____

2 marks

PS **3** Ari completes this calculation: 6432 + 3826 = 9258

Use an inverse calculation to check Ari's calculation. If it's wrong, correct the answer.

_____

1 mark

PS **4** Dino adds a number and 732, then subtracts 218 and reaches an answer of 861.

Write the number that Dino started with. _____

1 mark

Marks.......... /5

Total marks .... /19

How am I doing?

29

Addition and Subtraction Problems

PS Problem-solving questions

Challenge 1

PS **1** In a school, there are 286 children in Key Stage 2 and 139 children in Key Stage 1.

a) How many more children are there in Key Stage 2 than in Key Stage 1?

_____ children

b) How many children are there in Key Stages 1 and 2 altogether?

_____ children

2 marks

PS **2** A town has two car parks. One car park holds 327 cars; the other holds 286 cars.

How many parking spaces are there altogether? _____ spaces

1 mark

PS **3** Nisha chooses between two digital devices. One costs £439 and the other costs £385.

What is the difference in price between the two devices? £ _____

£439   £385

1 mark

PS **4** Nino is 161 cm tall. His brother is 36 cm shorter.

How tall is Nino's brother? _____ cm

1 mark

Marks.......... /5

Challenge 2

PS **1** Work out the number that is 3965 greater than 2832. _____

1 mark

PS **2** A theatre group gave two shows. In the afternoon, there were 1568 people in the audience and in the evening there were 1735 people.

How many people watched the two performances? _____ people

1 mark

Addition and Subtraction Problems

PS | **3** | Noah went on holiday. He drove 864 km from London to the south of France. He drove 365 km whilst on holiday and then he drove back to London.

How many kilometres did he drive altogether? _____ km

1 mark

PS | **4** | A shop has a stock of 3475 t-shirts. It sells 1294 t-shirts.

How many t-shirts does it have left? _____ t-shirts

1 mark

Marks.......... /4

Challenge 3

PS | **1** | Write the missing numbers in these calculations.

a)

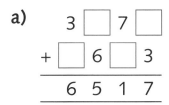

$$
\begin{array}{ccccc}
 & 3 & \Box & 7 & \Box \\
+ & \Box & 6 & \Box & 3 \\
\hline
 & 6 & 5 & 1 & 7 \\
\end{array}
$$

b)

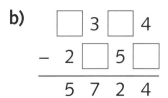

$$
\begin{array}{ccccc}
 & \Box & 3 & \Box & 4 \\
- & 2 & \Box & 5 & \Box \\
\hline
 & 5 & 7 & 2 & 4 \\
\end{array}
$$

2 marks

PS | **2** | Here are six number cards:

Use the cards to complete this calculation.

= 840

1 mark

PS | **3** | Work out these calculations and circle the one with the greatest answer.

A	5236 + 1609 = _____
B	9343 – 2434 = _____
C	2354 + 4567 = _____

4 marks

Marks.......... /7

Total marks .... /16 | How am I doing?

31

Multiplication and Division Facts

Challenge 1

1 Write the answers to:

a) 7 × 5 = _____

b) 3 × 8 = _____

c) 11 × 8 = _____

d) 12 × 3 = _____

e) 7 × 10 = _____

f) 8 × 4 = _____

6 marks

2 Fill in the missing numbers.

a) 4 × _____ = 28

b) 5 × _____ = 60

c) 3 × _____ = 21

d) _____ × 8 = 48

e) _____ × 10 = 100

f) _____ × 4 = 24

6 marks

3 Write the answers to:

a) 16 ÷ 2 = _____

b) 45 ÷ 5 = _____

c) 36 ÷ 4 = _____

d) 56 ÷ 8 = _____

e) 18 ÷ 3 = _____

f) 48 ÷ 4 = _____

6 marks

Marks......... /18

Challenge 2

1 Write the answers to:

a) 7 × 6 = _____

b) 4 × 7 = _____

c) 9 × 11 = _____

d) 8 × 7 = _____

e) 9 × 9 = _____

f) 12 × 7 = _____

6 marks

2 Fill in the missing numbers.

a) 7 × _____ = 49

b) 9 × _____ = 72

c) 6 × _____ = 72

d) _____ × 9 = 108

e) _____ × 12 = 144

f) _____ × 7 = 63

6 marks

Multiplication and Division Facts

3 Write the answers to:

a) $121 \div 11 =$ _____

b) $27 \div 9 =$ _____

c) $66 \div 6 =$ _____

d) $96 \div 8 =$ _____

e) $54 \div 9 =$ _____

f) $36 \div 9 =$ _____

6 marks

Marks......... /18

Challenge 3

PS **1** Complete the multiplication squares.

a)

×	7	9	12
7	49		
9			
12			

b)

×		8	
6	42		
		64	
	84		108

7 marks

PS **2** Use different whole numbers only to complete these multiplication facts.

a) $6 \times 8 =$ _____ $\times$ _____

b) $4 \times 9 =$ _____ $\times$ _____

c) $3 \times 8 =$ _____ $\times$ _____

d) $6 \times 12 =$ _____ $\times$ _____

4 marks

PS **3** Use whole numbers only to complete these division facts.

a) $54 \div 6 =$ _____ $\div 9$

b) $64 \div 8 =$ _____ $\div 7$

c) $96 \div 12 =$ _____ $\div 8$

d) $132 \div 11 =$ _____ $\div 10$

4 marks

Marks......... /15

Total marks .... /51   How am I doing?

Mental Multiplication and Division

Challenge 1

1 Write the answers to:

a) 5 × 1 = _____ b) 10 × 0 = _____ c) 0 × 8 = _____

d) 20 × 3 = _____ e) 40 × 4 = _____ f) 70 × 5 = _____

6 marks

2 Fill in the missing numbers.

a) _____ × 5 = 100 b) _____ × 4 = 80

c) _____ × 3 = 90

3 marks

3 Write the answers to:

a) 80 ÷ 2 = _____ b) 150 ÷ 5 = _____

c) 200 ÷ 4 = _____

3 marks

4 Fill in the missing numbers.

a) 180 ÷ _____ = 60

b) 250 ÷ _____ = 50

c) 160 ÷ _____ = 40

3 marks

Marks......... /15

Challenge 2

1 Write the answers to:

a) 15 × 2 = _____ b) 22 × 5 = _____ c) 16 × 4 = _____

d) 23 × 3 = _____ e) 32 × 4 = _____ f) 51 × 5 = _____

6 marks

2 Write the answers to:

a) 45 ÷ 3 = _____ b) 52 ÷ 4 = _____ c) 70 ÷ 5 = _____

d) 68 ÷ 2 = _____ e) 64 ÷ 4 = _____ f) 66 ÷ 3 = _____

6 marks

Mental Multiplication and Division

3 Write the answers to:

a) 4 × 2 × 6 = _____

b) 5 × 2 × 9 = _____

c) 6 × 2 × 6 = _____

3 marks

Marks......... /15

Challenge 3

1 Fill in the missing numbers.

a) 23 × _____ = 69

b) 32 × _____ = 128

c) 51 × _____ = 255

d) 53 × _____ = 159

e) 24 × _____ = 120

f) 82 × _____ = 246

6 marks

2 Fill in the missing numbers.

a) 3 × 5 × _____ = 45

b) 4 × _____ × 5 = 120

c) _____ × 10 × 2 = 80

d) 7 × 3 × _____ = 84

e) 2 × _____ × 2 = 48

f) _____ × 3 × 8 = 72

6 marks

3 Fill in the missing numbers.

a) 12 × 6 = 6 × 3 × _____

b) 15 × 6 = 6 × 5 × _____

c) _____ × 8 = 8 × 5 × 3

d) _____ × 7 = 7 × 8 × 3

4 marks

Marks......... /16

Total marks .... /46   How am I doing?

35

Factors

PS Problem-solving questions

Challenge 1

1 Circle the true statements.

A 6 is a factor of 12	**B** 4 is a factor of 18
C 15 is a factor of 5	**D** 8 is a factor of 24
E 3 is a factor of 35	**F** 9 is a factor of 72

3 marks

2 Write the missing numbers.

a) $5 \times 7 = 7 \times$ _____

b) $12 \times 4 = 4 \times$ _____

2 marks

3 Write the missing factor of 36.

4   36   6   2   18   3   12   1   _____

1 mark

PS **4** Circle the factors of 30.

1   3   4   5   8   10   12   15

1 mark

Marks.........../7

Challenge 2

1 Write all the factors of:

a) 10 _____

b) 21 _____

c) 32 _____

d) 40 _____

4 marks

2 Write the missing factor pair of 42.

1 and 42	3 and 14	6 and 7	_____ and _____

1 mark

3 Write the missing factor pair of 56.

1 and 56	2 and 28	4 and 14	_____ and _____

1 mark

Factors

4 Circle any correct statements.

A $8 \div 9 = 9 \div 8$ B $12 \times 11 = 11 \times 12$

1 mark

PS **5** I think of a number greater than 6. It is a factor of both 28 and 49.

What is my number?   _____

1 mark

Marks.........../8

Challenge 3

1 Write these numbers in the Venn diagram.

4   5   6   8   10

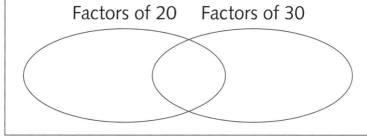

Factors of 20   Factors of 30

5 marks

PS **2** Faisal says, "I have a crate of bottles. There are 8 rows of 6 bottles."

Faisal can also say, "I have a crate of bottles. There are _____

rows of _____ bottles."

1 mark

3 List the factor pairs of:

a) 48   _____

b) 60   _____

c) 100   _____

3 marks

4 Write the factors of 56 that are not factors of 28. _____

1 mark

Marks........../10

Total marks ..../25   How am I doing?

37

Multiplication Practice

 PS Problem-solving questions

Challenge 1

1 Calculate these multiplications.

a)   4 6   b)   5 3   c)   6 2   d)   3 7
   ×   5   ×   6   ×   4   ×   3
   ─────────   ─────────   ─────────   ─────────

   ─────────   ─────────   ─────────   ─────────

 4 marks

2 Set out these problems using column multiplication and calculate.

a) 36 × 6 =	b) 72 × 5 =	c) 84 × 8 =

3 marks

3 Write in the missing numbers.

a) 57 × 4 = 50 × 4 + 7 × _____ = 228

b) 73 × _____ = 70 × 3 + 3 × 3 = 219

 2 marks

Marks.......... /9

Challenge 2

1 Calculate these multiplications.

a)   2 5 3   b)   6 0 7   c)   6 3 7
   ×   6   ×   5   ×   7
   ─────────────   ─────────────   ─────────────

   ─────────────   ─────────────   ─────────────

 3 marks

2 Write in the missing numbers.

a) 725 × 6 = 700 × _____ + 20 × _____ + 5 × _____ = 4350

b) 321 × 4 = 642 × _____

 2 marks

Multiplication Practice

3 Set out these problems using column multiplication and calculate.

a) 427 × 7 =	**b)** 683 × 6 =	**c)** 427 × 9 =

3 marks

Marks.......... /8

Challenge 3

1 Set out these problems using column multiplication and calculate.

a) 856 × 7 =	**b)** 967 × 8 =	**c)** 956 × 9 =

3 marks

PS **2** Fill in the missing numbers.

a)
```
  [ ] 4 [ ]
×       7
─────────
  3 8 2 9
```

b)
```
  [ ] 8 [ ]
×       9
─────────
  3 4 6 5
```

c)
```
  [ ] 7 [ ]
×       8
─────────
  2 2 0 8
```

3 marks

PS **3** Nishi has four number cards. She arranges them into a multiplication.

3   4   6   6

Fill in the multiplication on the right to find the largest total Nishi can make.

1 mark

Marks.......... /7

Total marks .... /24   How am I doing?

Multiplication Problems

PS Problem-solving questions

Challenge 1

PS **1** There are 48 bottles in a crate.

How many bottles will there be in 6 crates? _____ bottles

1 mark

PS **2** Jack has 35 marbles in a bag. He has 8 similar bags.

How many marbles does he have altogether? _____ marbles

1 mark

PS **3** Jess buys 3 packs of apples. There are 15 apples altogether.

How many apples will there be in 12 packs? _____ apples

1 mark

PS **4** A pack of 4 tins of beans costs £1.75.

How much would you pay for 20 tins of beans? £_____

1 mark

PS **5** There are 6 classes in a school. Each class has 28 children.

How many children are in the school? _____ children

1 mark

Marks.......... /5

Challenge 2

PS **1** A farmer keeps 186 chickens. Each chicken lays 4 eggs a week.

How many eggs are laid in a week? _____ eggs

1 mark

PS **2** A sack of tulip bulbs holds 256 bulbs. Dave plants 6 sacks of bulbs.

How many bulbs has Dave planted? _____ bulbs

1 mark

PS **3** A shop sells 3 televisions that cost £375 each and 7 televisions that cost £435 each.

What is the total cost of the televisions? £_____

1 mark

Multiplication Problems

 4 A school puts on a show in the school hall.
It sells 278 tickets for each performance.
There are 5 performances.

How many tickets are sold? _____ tickets

1 mark

5 A teacher buys 8 jars of counters. Each jar holds 475 counters.

How many counters are there altogether? _____ counters

1 mark

Marks.......... /5

Challenge 3

1 This table shows the cost of different air fares from London.

To From	New York	Los Angeles	Dubai	New Delhi	Sydney
London (One way)	£346	£465	£486	£518	£648
London (Return)	£452	£573	£549	£647	£732

What is the cost of:

a) 5 one-way tickets to Dubai? £_____

b) 4 return tickets to Sydney? £_____

c) 6 one-way tickets to Los Angeles? £_____

d) 8 return tickets to New Delhi? £_____

e) 7 one-way tickets to New York? £_____

5 marks

Marks.......... /5

Total marks .... /15

How am I doing?

Progress Test 1

1. Write the next numbers in the sequences.

   a) | 48 | 54 | 60 | 66 | | |

   b) | 775 | 800 | 825 | 850 | | |

2 marks

2. Write these numbers in order, starting with the smallest.

   5724   5274   5472   5427   5742

   _____   _____   _____   _____   _____

1 mark

3. Write < or > in the circles to make each number sentence correct.

   a) 7903 ◯ 7907   b) 5634 ◯ 5833

2 marks

PS ⟩ 4. A car is for sale and costs £8799. The car dealer reduces the price by £1000.

   What is the reduced price of the car?   £_____

1 mark

5. Work out:

   a) 6835 – 1000 = _____   b) 4008 + 1000 = _____

2 marks

6. Circle the number in which the digit 2 has a value of two thousand.

   4285   5629   2390   6132   7264

1 mark

PS ⟩ 7. Sunil has these number cards.

   Use the cards to make the
   largest possible number
   with three hundreds.   _____

3   5   4   8

1 mark

8. Write these Roman numerals as numbers.

   a) XXXVIII = _____

   b) LXIV = _____

2 marks

42

9. These Roman numerals are written as a calculation: XXXV + VII = ?
   Circle the correct answer.

   LXII   **XLIIIV**   **LII**   **XLII**

10. Write the three-digit number represented by these blocks. _____

11. Write the numbers the arrows point to.

    a) _____   b) _____

    0   100   200

12. Round each number to the nearest 100.

    a) 528 _____   b) 761 _____   c) 89 _____

13. Complete this table by rounding the number to the nearest 10, 100 and 1000.

	Rounded to the nearest 10 is	Rounded to the nearest 100 is	Rounded to the nearest 1000 is
5826			

14. Write the next two numbers in this sequence.

PS 15. Flo counts back in fives from 20.

    Write the first number below zero she counts. _____

16. Work out:

    a)   4 2 7   b)   7 9 5   c)   8 1 5
        − 1 8 7   + 2 8 5   − 2 7 0
        _____   _____   _____

    _____   _____   _____

PS ⟩ **17.** Write in the missing numbers.

a)
```
    5 □ 7
  - □ 5 □
  ─────────
    1 7 4
```

b)
```
    □ 5 □
  + 5 □ 1
  ─────────
    9 0 9
```

2 marks

18. Circle the calculation that is the inverse of $694 - 322 = 372$

| 372 + 694 | 694 – 322 | 372 + 322 | 372 – 322 |

1 mark

PS ⟩ **19.** Sven completes the calculation shown on the right. He then works out the inverse calculation to check his work.

```
    3 8 2
  + 4 6 5
  ─────────
    7 4 7
```

Write the answer to Sven's inverse calculation. _____

1 mark

PS ⟩ **20.** Ivete has 275 minutes talk time left on her phone. She uses up another 126 minutes and then her monthly allowance increases the talk time by 450 minutes.

How many minutes does Ivete have on her phone now? _____ minutes

1 mark

PS ⟩ **21.** Tarun has to drive 356 kilometres. After 186 kilometres he stops to have lunch and then, after another 137 kilometres, he stops for a coffee.

How much further does Tarun have to drive? _____ kilometres

1 mark

22. Work out:

a) $5 \times 7 = $ _____   b) $3 \times 9 = $ _____   c) $7 \times 12 = $ _____

d) $48 \div 6 = $ _____   e) $144 \div 12 = $ _____   f) $54 \div 9 = $ _____

6 marks

PS ⟩ **23.** Write the missing numbers in this multiplication square.

×	6	9	
4	24	36	48
		81	
7	42	63	84

2 marks

44

24. Work out:

a) $15 \times 5 = $ _____ **b)** $48 \div 3 = $ _____

c) $22 \times 4 = $ _____ **d)** $72 \div 4 = $ _____

e) $96 \div 8 = $ _____ **f)** $17 \times 6 = $ _____

 6 marks

25. Write the factor pairs of:

a) 20 _____

b) 100 _____

 2 marks

26. Work out:

a)
```
    6 3
×     6
───────

───────
```
b)
```
  2 6 5
×     4
───────

───────
```
c)
```
  6 0 8
×     7
───────

───────
```

 3 marks

PS **27.** A school has 8 classes and each class can hold 30 children. There are 216 children in the school.

How many spare places are there? _____ spare places

 1 mark

28. Fill in the missing numbers.

$54 \times 3 = 50 \times 3 + $ _____ $\times$ _____ $= 162$

 1 mark

PS **29.** A factory uses 7 metres of wood to make a wardrobe.

How much wood is needed to make 5 wardrobes? _____ metres

 1 mark

30. Michael completes 3 tests worth a total of 50 marks.

How many marks are available if he completes 6 tests?

_____ marks

 1 mark

Marks........ /56

Hundredths

PS ⟩ Problem-solving questions

Challenge 1

1 What fraction is shown by each drawing?

a) _____   b) _____   c) _____

3 marks

2 Write in the missing fractions.

a)

$\frac{7}{100}$ $\frac{8}{100}$ ☐ $\frac{10}{100}$ $\frac{11}{100}$ $\frac{12}{100}$

b)

$\frac{77}{100}$ $\frac{78}{100}$ ☐ ☐ ☐ $\frac{82}{100}$ $\frac{83}{100}$

2 marks

3 Complete this sentence:

When 1 is divided by _____ the answer is $\frac{1}{100}$.

1 mark

Marks.......... /6

Challenge 2

1 What fraction is shown by each drawing?

a) _____   b) _____   c) _____

3 marks

2 Divide each number by 100. Give your answers as fractions.

a) 6 _____   b) 9 _____   c) 2 _____

3 marks

46

Hundredths

PS | 3 Kesha has a 5 litre bottle of juice. This is exactly enough juice to make 100 drinks.

How much juice is used in each drink? Give your answer as a fraction of a litre.

_____

1 mark

PS | 4 How many centimetres are in $\frac{1}{100}$ of a metre? _____ cm

1 mark

Marks.......... /8

Challenge 3

1 Circle the calculation with the correct answer.

$50 \div 100 = \frac{5}{100}$

$5 \div 100 = \frac{5}{10}$

$500 \div 100 = \frac{5}{100}$

$5 \div 100 = \frac{5}{100}$

1 mark

2 Circle both calculations that have an answer of $\frac{1}{100}$.

$1 \div 10$ $1 \div 100$ $0.1 \div 10$ $0.1 \div 100$

2 marks

3 Write in the missing numbers.

a) _____ $\div 100 = \frac{7}{100}$

b) _____ $\div 100 = \frac{5}{100}$

c) _____ $\div 10 = \frac{7}{100}$

3 marks

4 Write in the missing numbers.

a) $0.6 \div 10 =$ _____ $\div 100$

b) $0.7 \div$ _____ $= 7 \div 100$

2 marks

Marks.......... /8

Total marks .... /22 How am I doing?

47

Equivalent Fractions

PS ⟩ Problem-solving questions

Challenge 1

1 Fill in the missing equivalent fractions shown by the drawings.

a) ☐☐ = ☐☐   b) ☐☐☐ = ☐☐

_____ = _____   _____ = _____

2 marks

2 Use the fraction bars to complete the equivalent fractions.

one whole
halves
fifths
tenths

a) $\frac{1}{2} = \frac{\square}{10}$ b) $\frac{3}{5} = \frac{\square}{10}$ c) $\frac{4}{5} = \frac{\square}{10}$

3 marks

3 Use the diagrams to help you complete the equivalent fractions.

a)   b)   c)

$\frac{1}{2} = \frac{4}{\square}$ $\frac{1}{3} = \frac{2}{\square}$ $\frac{\square}{4} = \frac{6}{8}$

3 marks

Marks.......... /8

Challenge 2

1 This rectangle is divided into twentieths.

Use the diagram to help you complete the equivalent fractions.

a) $\frac{1}{2} = \frac{\square}{20}$ b) $\frac{3}{10} = \frac{\square}{20}$ c) $\frac{3}{5} = \frac{\square}{20}$

3 marks

Equivalent Fractions

2 This rectangle is divided into fifteenths.
Use the diagram to help you complete the
equivalent fractions.

a) $\frac{1}{3} = \frac{\boxed{}}{15}$ b) $\frac{2}{3} = \frac{\boxed{}}{15}$ c) $\frac{3}{5} = \frac{\boxed{}}{15}$

3 marks

3 Here are families of equivalent fractions. Complete the fractions.

a) $\frac{1}{3} = \frac{2}{6} = \frac{3}{9} = \frac{\boxed{}}{12} = \frac{5}{\boxed{}} = \frac{\boxed{}}{18} = \frac{7}{\boxed{}} = \frac{\boxed{}}{24}$

b) $\frac{3}{4} = \frac{6}{8} = \frac{9}{12} = \frac{\boxed{}}{16} = \frac{15}{\boxed{}} = \frac{\boxed{}}{24} = \frac{21}{\boxed{}} = \frac{\boxed{}}{32}$

2 marks

Marks.......... /8

Challenge 3

1 Use the fraction bars to help you complete the equivalent fractions.

one whole
halves
quarters
fifths
tenths
twentieths

a) $\frac{1}{2} = \frac{\boxed{}}{20}$ b) $\frac{4}{5} = \frac{\boxed{}}{20}$ c) $\frac{3}{10} = \frac{\boxed{}}{20}$

d) $\frac{\boxed{}}{4} = \frac{5}{20}$ e) $\frac{\boxed{}}{5} = \frac{8}{20}$ f) $\frac{\boxed{}}{10} = \frac{18}{20}$

6 marks

2 Circle both fractions that are **not** equivalent to $\frac{1}{4}$.

$\frac{3}{12}$ $\frac{5}{20}$ $\frac{8}{30}$ $\frac{12}{48}$ $\frac{15}{60}$ $\frac{20}{100}$

2 marks

 3 There are 10 cans of paint. 4 of the cans are blue paint.

Complete this sentence: $\frac{2}{\boxed{}}$ of the cans of paint are blue.

1 mark

Marks.......... /9

Total marks .... /25   How am I doing?

49

Addition and Subtraction of Fractions

Challenge 1

1 Complete these calculations.

Example: ☐☐☐☐ + ☐☐☐☐ =

$\frac{1}{4}$ + $\frac{2}{4}$ = $\frac{3}{4}$

a) ☐☐☐☐☐ + ☐☐☐☐☐ =

_____ + _____ = _____

b) ☐☐☐☐☐☐ – ☐☐☐☐☐☐ =

_____ – _____ = _____

2 marks

2 Work out the answers to these calculations.

a) $\frac{2}{3} + \frac{1}{3}$ = _____   b) $\frac{7}{8} + \frac{6}{8}$ = _____   c) $\frac{8}{10} + \frac{9}{10}$ = _____

3 marks

3 Work out the answers to these calculations.

a) $\frac{4}{5} - \frac{1}{5}$ = _____   b) $\frac{9}{10} - \frac{6}{10}$ = _____   c) $\frac{7}{8} - \frac{6}{8}$ = _____

3 marks

Marks.......... /8

Challenge 2

1 Complete these calculations.

Example: ☐☐☐☐ + ☐☐☐☐ =

$\frac{3}{4}$ + $\frac{2}{4}$ = $\frac{5}{4}$ = $1\frac{1}{4}$

a) ☐☐☐☐☐ + ☐☐☐☐☐ =

_____ + _____ = _____ = _____

b) ☐☐☐☐☐☐ + ☐☐☐☐☐☐ =

_____ + _____ = _____ = _____

2 marks

Addition and Subtraction of Fractions

2 Work out the answers to these calculations.

a) $\frac{2}{3} + \frac{2}{3} =$ _____ = _____

b) $\frac{3}{5} + \frac{4}{5} =$ _____ = _____

c) $\frac{3}{4} + \frac{3}{4} =$ _____ = _____

3 marks

3 Work out the answers to these calculations.

a) $\frac{9}{10} - \frac{6}{10} =$ _____

b) $\frac{9}{12} - \frac{4}{12} =$ _____

c) $\frac{15}{10} - \frac{6}{10} =$ _____

3 marks

Marks.......... /8

Challenge 3

1 Write in the missing fractions.

a) – ? =

_____ – _____ = _____

b) + ? =

_____ + _____ = _____ = _____

2 marks

2 Write the missing fractions in these calculations.

a) $\frac{2}{10} +$ _____ $= \frac{7}{10}$ b) $\frac{3}{12} +$ _____ $= \frac{9}{12}$ c) _____ $+ \frac{1}{8} = 1\frac{2}{8}$

3 marks

3 Write the missing fractions in these calculations.

a) $\frac{7}{8} -$ _____ $= \frac{2}{8}$ b) _____ $- \frac{2}{7} = \frac{4}{7}$

c) $\frac{8}{10} -$ _____ $= \frac{5}{10}$

3 marks

Marks.......... /8

Total marks .... /24   How am I doing?

Finding Fractions

Challenge 1

1 Work out:

a) $\frac{1}{3}$ of 15 = _____

b) $\frac{1}{4}$ of 24 = _____

c) $\frac{1}{6}$ of 36 m = _____ m

d) $\frac{1}{8}$ of 32 kg = _____ kg

4 marks

2 Work out:

a) $\frac{2}{3}$ of 24 = _____

b) $\frac{4}{5}$ of 20 = _____

c) $\frac{3}{4}$ of 36 ml = _____ ml

d) $\frac{2}{2}$ of 25 km = _____ km

4 marks

PS **3** Lesa is on a sponsored run. The run is 12 kilometres. Lesa has completed $\frac{1}{6}$ of the course.

How far has she run? _____ km

1 mark

PS **4** There are 28 children in a class. $\frac{1}{2}$ of the class are boys.

How many girls are in the class? _____

1 mark

Marks......... /10

Challenge 2

1 Work out:

a) $\frac{1}{10}$ of 70 = _____

b) $\frac{1}{7}$ of 28 = _____

c) $\frac{1}{12}$ of £24 = £_____

d) $\frac{1}{15}$ of 30 m = _____ m

4 marks

2 Work out:

a) $\frac{2}{5}$ of 35 = _____

b) $\frac{7}{8}$ of 32 = _____

c) $\frac{11}{12}$ of 60 cm = _____ cm

d) $\frac{3}{20}$ of 40 km = _____ km

4 marks

PS **3** Cath has a 40 kilogram bag of coal. She has used $\frac{3}{5}$ of the bag.

How much coal has she used? _____ kg

1 mark

Finding Fractions

4 This bar is divided into fifths, but part of the bar is hidden. The value of each fifth is shown.

| 6 | 6 | |

What is the value of the whole bar? _____

1 mark

Marks......... /10

Challenge 3

1 Work out: **a)** $\frac{7}{12}$ of 60 = _____ **b)** $\frac{5}{9}$ of 81 = _____

2 marks

 2 A gift shop sells 40 pens. $\frac{2}{5}$ of the pens have blue ink and $\frac{3}{8}$ of the pens have black ink. The rest have red ink.

How many pens have red ink? _____

1 mark

3 Write in the missing numbers.

a) $\frac{3}{4}$ of _____ = 15 **b)** $\frac{3}{10}$ of _____ = 9

2 marks

4 Work out $\frac{3}{2}$ of 10. _____

1 mark

 5 There are 27 children in a class. Jo says, "$\frac{1}{2}$ of the class are girls and $\frac{1}{2}$ of the class are boys."

Explain why Jo must be wrong.

_____

_____

1 mark

6 Work out the missing numbers.

a) $\frac{3}{4}$ of _____ = $\frac{1}{8}$ of 24 **b)** $\frac{3}{5}$ of _____ = $\frac{3}{4}$ of 16

2 marks

Marks......... /9

Total marks .... /29　　　　How am I doing?

53

Fraction and Decimal Equivalents

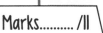 Problem-solving questions

Challenge 1

1 Draw lines to match each fraction to the equivalent decimal.

$\frac{3}{4}$ $\frac{1}{2}$ $\frac{1}{4}$

0.5   0.75   0.25

1 mark

2 Write these fractions as decimals.

a) $\frac{1}{10}$ = _____   b) $\frac{7}{10}$ = _____   c) $\frac{3}{10}$ = _____

3 marks

3 Write as decimals:

a) Nine tenths = _____   b) One and six tenths = _____

c) Two and four tenths = _____ d) Five and five tenths = _____

4 marks

4 Here is a number line.
Write the numbers that the arrows are pointing to.

a) _____   b) _____ c) _____

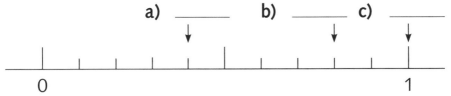

0   1

3 marks

Marks......... /11

Challenge 2

1 Write these fractions as decimals.

a) $\frac{1}{2}$ = _____   b) $\frac{1}{4}$ = _____   c) $\frac{3}{4}$ = _____

3 marks

2 Write these fractions as decimals.

a) $\frac{9}{10}$ = _____   b) $\frac{57}{100}$ = _____   c) $\frac{3}{100}$ = _____

3 marks

Fraction and Decimal Equivalents

 3 Gia says, "I have got four pounds and fifty-seven pence."

What is the usual way to write this using digits? _____

1 mark

4 Here is a number line.
Write the decimals that the arrows are pointing to.

3 marks

Marks......... /10

Challenge 3

1 Write these fractions as decimals.

a) $\frac{9}{100}$ = _____   b) $\frac{20}{100}$ = _____   c) $\frac{101}{100}$ = _____

3 marks

2 Estimate the decimals that the arrows are pointing to.

3 marks

 3 Look at what James says.
Explain why he is incorrect.

_____

_____

_____

$\frac{7}{100}$ is 0.7

1 mark

4 Write in the missing numbers.

a) $\frac{3}{10}$ = 0.03 × _____   b) $\frac{70}{100}$ = 0.07 × _____

2 marks

Marks.......... /9

Total marks .... /30   How am I doing?

55

Rounding Decimals

PS⟩ Problem-solving questions

Challenge 1

1 Round each decimal to the nearest whole number.

a) 5.1 _____   b) 4.8 _____   c) 2.9 _____

d) 6.4 _____   e) 7.6 _____   f) 3.3 _____

6 marks

PS **2** Zain cut a length of wood. It was 2.7 metres long.

Write the length of the wood to the nearest metre. _____ m

1 mark

PS **3** A jug is filled with 1.2 litres of drink.

Write the capacity to the nearest litre. _____ litre(s)

1 mark

PS **4** Kat thinks of a decimal number between 6 and 7. She rounds her number to the nearest whole number. The answer is 7.

Write what Kat's number could have been. _____

1 mark

Marks.......... /9

Challenge 2

1 Round each decimal to the nearest whole number.

a) 7.4 _____   b) 6.5 _____   c) 21.8 _____

d) 53.7 _____   e) 86.3 _____   f) 105.3 _____

6 marks

PS **2** Sam weighs 49.6 kilograms.

Write this mass to the nearest kilogram. _____ kg

1 mark

PS **3** Tiana rounds a number to the nearest whole number. The answer is 50.

Write what Tiana's number could have been.

_____

1 mark

Rounding Decimals

PS **4** Debbie rounds numbers to the nearest whole number.
Circle the numbers she will round to 30.

30.6   32.1   29.7   30.4   29.3

2 marks

Marks......... /10

Challenge 3

1 Round each decimal to the nearest whole number.

a) 116.3 _____   b) 229.8 _____   c) 707.0 _____

3 marks

PS **2** Scott rounds numbers to the nearest whole number.
Circle the numbers he will round to 100.

98.9   100.3   99.6   100.9   99.1

2 marks

PS **3** Fay adds 6.2 and 7.4 together.
She estimates the answer by rounding each number to the nearest whole.

Write the total of the rounded numbers.   _____

1 mark

PS **4** Aaron rounds numbers to the nearest whole number.
Draw lines to match the decimal numbers to the rounded numbers.

48.7   49.8   50.4   49.5   49.4

49   50

1 mark

1 mark

Marks......... /7

Total marks .... /26   How am I doing?

Comparing Decimals

Challenge 1

1 Circle the largest decimal number.

0.4   0.8   0.2   0.7

1 mark

2 Circle the smallest decimal number.

2.4   2.8   3.1   2.5

1 mark

3 Write these decimal numbers in order, starting with the smallest.

5.6   6.2   5.9   4.7

_____   _____   _____   _____

1 mark

PS **4** George has £3.56, Raja has £5, Craig has £7.32 and Obe has £4.98.

Write who has the most money.   _____

1 mark

PS **5** Write a decimal between 7.6 and 8.   _____

1 mark

Marks.......... /5

Challenge 2

1 Circle the largest decimal in this list.

5.89   6.25   12.16   8.99   3.75

1 mark

2 Write these decimals in order, starting with the smallest.

34.45   45.43   45.34   35.44   43.54

_____   _____   _____   _____   _____

1 mark

Comparing Decimals

PS **3** Ned puts these decimals in order, starting with the smallest.

 60.05 60.56 66.06 65.66 60.06

Write the decimal that is third in Ned's list. _____

1 mark

4 Write a decimal between 23.56 and 23.62 _____

1 mark

5 Akash orders five numbers. Write what the missing numbers could be.

45.43 > _____ > 45.34 > _____ > 45.27

2 marks

Marks.......... /6

Challenge 3

1 Put the correct symbol < or > in each circle.

a) 5.67 ◯ 6.57   **b)** 23.56 ◯ 23.46

2 marks

PS **2** Jay has five pieces of wood. They are 3.25 m, 3.76 m, 2.88 m, 3.75 m and 2.98 m long.

a) Write the longest length. _____ m

b) Write the shortest length. _____ m

2 marks

3 5.6 and 5.7 are shown on this number line.

Mark 4.8 and 6.2 on the number line.

5.6 5.7

2 marks

4 Write these numbers in order, smallest first.

52.5   **5.25**   **6**   **50**   **25.5**

_____ _____ _____ _____ _____

1 mark

Marks.......... /7

Total marks .... /18   How am I doing?

59

Dividing by 10 and 100

PS Problem-solving questions

Challenge 1

1 Complete these calculations.

a) $6 \div 10 =$ _____

b) $12 \div 10 =$ _____

c) $0.7 \div 10 =$ _____

d) $2.5 \div 10 =$ _____

4 marks

2 Fill in the missing numbers.

a) _____ $\div 10 = 0.5$

b) _____ $\div 10 = 3.6$

c) _____ $\div 10 = 0.63$

3 marks

3 Write the value of the 7 in the answer of each calculation.

a) $7 \div 10 =$ _____

b) $70 \div 10 =$ _____

c) $0.7 \div 10 =$ _____

3 marks

PS **4** A 2.5 kg bag of dog food is enough for 10 meals.

How much dog food is used for each meal? _____ kg

1 mark

Marks.......... /11

Challenge 2

1 Complete these calculations.

a) $6.7 \div 10 =$ _____

b) $54 \div 100 =$ _____

c) $15 \div 100 =$ _____

d) $78 \div 10 =$ _____

4 marks

2 Fill in the missing numbers.

a) _____ $\div 10 = 0.57$

b) _____ $\div 10 = 3.6$

c) $92 \div$ _____ $= 0.92$

d) $46 \div$ _____ $= 0.46$

4 marks

PS **3** Sunita divides a number by 100. The answer is six tenths.

Write the number Sunita divided. _____

1 mark

Dividing by 10 and 100

4 Write the value of the 4 in the answer of each calculation.

a) 34 ÷ 100 = _____   **b)** 6.4 ÷ 10 = _____

2 marks

PS **5** Gus buys 100 of the same stamps and pays £64 for them.

What is the cost of each stamp?   £ _____

1 mark

Marks......... /12

Challenge 3

1 Write in the missing numbers.

a) 12 ÷ _____ = 1.2   **b)** 27 ÷ _____ = 0.27

c) _____ ÷ 10 = 3.2   **d)** _____ ÷ 100 = 0.79

4 marks

PS **2** Kagendo divides a number and works out the answer to be nine hundredths.
Sally divides the same number and works out the answer to be nine tenths.

Write what Kagendo's and Sally's calculations could have been.

Kagendo's calculation: _____

Sally's calculation: _____

2 marks

3 Circle the calculations that have answers with 6 tenths.

| 64 ÷ 10 | 56 ÷ 100 | 6.7 ÷ 10 | 56 ÷ 10 | 36 ÷ 100 |

2 marks

PS **4** Write division calculations dividing by 10.

a) _____ ÷ _____ = four ones and five tenths

b) _____ ÷ _____ = six ones and eight hundredths

2 marks

Marks......... /10

Total marks .... /33   How am I doing?

61

Decimal Problems

Challenge 1

PS **1** A shop sells the following items.

Pens £2.75   £1.25   £5.25   £4.95

a) Holly buys a set of pens, a ruler and a pencil case. What was the total cost? £_____

b) Josef has a £10 note. He buys a book. How much change does he get? £_____

c) Katie spent £7.70 on two items. Which two items did she buy?

_____   _____

3 marks

PS **2** Michelle has two bottles that each hold 4 litres of water. One is half full and the other is one-quarter full. How any litres of water does Michelle have? _____ litres

1 mark

PS **3** Obi lives 2500 metres from school. He walks to and from school five days a week. How far does he walk in one week walking to and from school? Give your answer in kilometres. _____ km

1 mark

PS **4** Oranges cost £1.20 per kilogram. Jane buys 2 kilograms of oranges. How much does she pay? £_____

1 mark

Marks.......... /6

Challenge 2

PS **1** Pippa has £50. She buys a dress for £19.90 and a pair of shoes for £24.99. How much money does Pippa have left? £_____

1 mark

PS **2** Bananas cost 70p per kilogram. Tim buys $1\frac{1}{2}$ kg of bananas. How much does he pay? £_____

1 mark

Decimal Problems

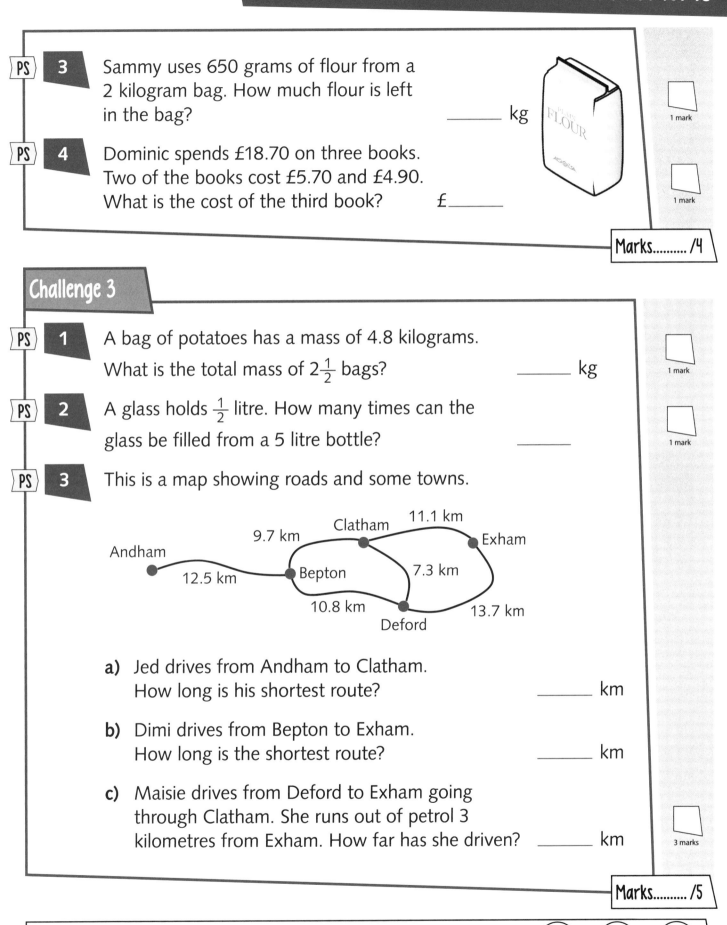

PS 3   Sammy uses 650 grams of flour from a 2 kilogram bag. How much flour is left in the bag?

_____ kg

1 mark

PS 4   Dominic spends £18.70 on three books. Two of the books cost £5.70 and £4.90. What is the cost of the third book?

£_____

1 mark

Marks.........../4

Challenge 3

PS 1   A bag of potatoes has a mass of 4.8 kilograms. What is the total mass of $2\frac{1}{2}$ bags?

_____ kg

1 mark

PS 2   A glass holds $\frac{1}{2}$ litre. How many times can the glass be filled from a 5 litre bottle?

_____

1 mark

PS 3   This is a map showing roads and some towns.

Andham — 12.5 km — Bepton
9.7 km — Clatham
11.1 km — Exham
7.3 km
10.8 km — Deford
13.7 km

a) Jed drives from Andham to Clatham. How long is his shortest route?

_____ km

b) Dimi drives from Bepton to Exham. How long is the shortest route?

_____ km

c) Maisie drives from Deford to Exham going through Clatham. She runs out of petrol 3 kilometres from Exham. How far has she driven?

_____ km

3 marks

Marks.........../5

Total marks ..../15   How am I doing?   😊 😐 😖

63

Progress Test 2

1. Write the next numbers in the sequences.

a)

49 | 56 | 63 | 70 | | |

b)
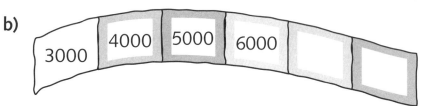

3000 | 4000 | 5000 | 6000 | | |

2 marks

2. Write these numbers in order, starting with the smallest.

8314   1834   1384   8341   4138

_____   _____   _____   _____   _____

1 mark

3. Circle the value of the digit 1 in the number 6914.

| 1 one | 1 ten | 1 hundred | 1 thousand |

1 mark

4. 538 can be written as 400 + 130 + 8.

Write 538 in two different ways.

a) _____   b) _____

2 marks

5. Complete the table by rounding each number to the nearest 10.

Number	Rounded to the nearest 10
3784	
427	
79	

3 marks

6. Write the next number in the sequence.

| 18 | 12 | 6 | 0 | |

1 mark

7. Work out:

   a) 6734 + 264 = _____   **b)** 5183 − 437 = _____

2 marks

8. Estimate the answer to 568 + 357 by rounding the numbers to the nearest hundred and adding the rounded numbers.

   _____ + _____ = _____

1 mark

PS 9. Josh buys and sells computer games. He has 387 games. He buys 56 games and sells 125 games.

How many computer games does he have now?   _____ games

1 mark

PS 10. Chloe has 65 metres of wood. She buys 120 more metres of wood to build a fence. She has 36 metres left over.

How much wood did Chloe use building the fence? _____ m

1 mark

11. Work out:

   a) $6 \times 4 \times 3 =$ _____   **b)** $5 \times 8 \times 6 =$ _____

2 marks

12. A factor pair of a number is 56 and 3.

What is the number? _____

1 mark

13. Work out:

   a)   5 3 2   **b)**   9 4 0   **c)**   6 2 8

      ×   4   ×   8   ×   6

3 marks

14. Write the missing numbers in this sentence:

2 children share 3 paint pots and 5 brushes, so 4 children share

_____ paint pots and _____ brushes.

2 marks

15. Write in the missing number: $48 \times 3 =$ _____ $\times 3 + 8 \times 3 = 144$

1 mark

16. Work out:

a) $3 \div 100 =$ _____

b) $9 \div 100 =$ _____

c) $\frac{7}{10} \div 10 =$ _____

3 marks

17. Estimate the fraction each arrow points to.

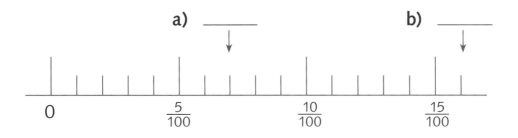

a) _____   b) _____

2 marks

18. a) $\frac{6}{8}$ of this circle is shaded. Write in the missing number.

$\frac{\square}{4}$ of this circle is shaded.

b) $\frac{1}{2}$ of this rectangle is shaded. Write in the missing number.

$\frac{\square}{10}$ of this rectangle is shaded.

2 marks

19. Work out:

a) $\frac{4}{10} + \frac{7}{10} =$ _____   b) $\frac{7}{8} + \frac{2}{8} =$ _____

2 marks

20. Write these decimals as fractions.

a) $0.13 =$ _____   b) $0.9 =$ _____   c) $0.09 =$ _____

3 marks

21. Write these fractions as decimals.

a) $\frac{93}{100} =$ _____   b) $\frac{7}{100} =$ _____   c) $\frac{4}{10} =$ _____

3 marks

22. Round each decimal to the nearest whole number.

 a) 4.7 _____   **b)** 15.4 _____   **c)** 29.8 _____

3 marks

PS **23.** Billy rounds a number, less than 25, with one decimal place to the nearest whole number. The rounded number is 25.

 What could Billy's number have been? _____

1 mark

24. Circle the largest number.

 73.8   9.3   20.0   68.9   73.7

1 mark

25. Write these numbers in order, starting with the smallest.

 31.6   **31.8**   **32.5**   **30.7**   **30.2**

 _____   _____   _____   _____   _____

1 mark

26. Write in the missing numbers.

 a) 5.6 ÷ _____ = 0.56   **b)** 9 ÷ _____ = 0.09

 c) 16 ÷ _____ = 0.16   **d)** 0.8 ÷ _____ = 0.08

4 marks

PS **27.** Chandra divides a two-digit number by 10. The answer has 5 ones and 7 tenths.

 What was the number that Chandra divided? _____

1 mark

28. Work out:

 a) $\frac{2}{5}$ of 25 = _____   **b)** $\frac{3}{4}$ of 32 = _____

 c) $\frac{9}{10}$ of 90 = _____

3 marks

29. Jade buys 4 t-shirts that cost £7.25 each.

 Work out the total cost of the 4 t-shirts.   £ _____

1 mark

Marks............/54

Measurement

Comparing Measures

Problem-solving questions

1 Write these lengths in order, longest first.

36.87 m 63.78 m 83.76 m 83.67 m 38.76 m

_____ _____ _____ _____ _____

1 mark

2 Write these capacities in order, smallest first.

45.78 litres 4.87 litres 5.47 litres 54.87 litres 78.54 litres

_____ _____ _____ _____ _____

1 mark

PS **3** Sonya has three different-sized jugs. The largest jug holds 4.75 litres and the smallest jug holds 4.56 litres.

What could the capacity of the third jug be? _____ litres

1 mark

4 There are three lengths of ribbon. The lengths are $1\frac{1}{2}$ metres, 1.25 metres and 1.65 metres.

Write the lengths in order, smallest first.

_____ m _____ m _____ m

1 mark

PS **5** Stan weighs 43.76 kg, Dubry weighs 46.73 kg and Tom weighs 45.87 kg.

Who is the heaviest? _____

1 mark

Marks.......... /5

1 Circle the larger mass.

a) 3.2 kg or 2800 g b) 7.8 kg or 8000 g

2 marks

2 Circle the shorter length.

a) 5.6 m or 474 cm b) 67 mm or 6 cm

2 marks

3 Circle the larger capacity.

a) 5.675 litres or 570 ml b) 8000 ml or 10 litres

2 marks

68

Comparing Measures

4 Write these lengths in order, shortest first.

475 cm	5 m	4800 mm	4.7 m

_____   _____   _____   _____

1 mark

PS **5** Alvin has a 5 kilogram bag of flour. He uses 255 grams. Has he used over half of the bag? _____

1 mark

Marks.......... /8

Challenge 3

1 Circle the longest length.

$4\frac{1}{2}$ m   4.6 m $4\frac{3}{4}$ m   4.8 m   4.2 m

1 mark

2 Circle the shortest length.

5.7 kilometres   4500 metres

4.85 kilometres   5000 metres

1 mark

3 Amy is offered four drinks. She wants the largest drink. Circle the drink she should choose.

300 ml can	0.5 litre bottle	0.25 litre glass	1 litre bottle

1 mark

PS **4** There are three parcels. Parcel A weighs 6 kg, parcel B is $\frac{1}{2}$ kg heavier than parcel A and parcel C is 250 g lighter than parcel B.

Write the parcels in order, the heaviest mass first.

_____   _____   _____

1 mark

Marks.......... /4

Total marks .... /17   How am I doing?

69

Estimating Measures

PS Problem-solving questions

Challenge 1

1 Estimate the mass of the parcel.

_____ kg

1 mark

2 Estimate the length of the line below. _____ cm

```
0   1   2   3   4   5   6   7   8   9   10
|ıııı|ıııı|ıııı|ıııı|ıııı|ıııı|ıııı|ıııı|ıııı|ıııı|
```

_____

1 mark

3 Estimate how much liquid is in the jug. _____ litre(s)

1 mark

4 Phil gets £50 to go shopping. At the end he says,
"I have about half of my money left."

Tick the amounts of money Phil could have.

(£45) (£24.75) (£36.50) (£26.15) (£0.50)

2 marks

Marks.......... /5

Challenge 2

1 Tick the best estimate for the length of a car.

| 40 mm | | 40 cm | | 4 m | | 0.4 km |

1 mark

2 Tick the best estimate for the capacity of a mug.

(35 ml) (35 litres) (350 ml) (3.5 litres)

1 mark

3 Tick the best estimate for the mass of a banana.

| 120 g | | 12 g | | 1.2 kg | | 12 kg |

1 mark

Estimating Measures

4 Melanie walks 1 kilometre to school with no stops.
Tick the best estimate for the time it will take.

| 1 minute | 12 minutes | 45 minutes | 1 hour |

1 mark

Marks.........../4

Challenge 3

1 Adam goes for a meal. He chooses the following items.

£7.60   £3.65   £2.55

Estimate the cost of the meal by rounding the prices to the nearest

pound and adding the rounded prices.   £ _____

1 mark

2 Estimate the temperature shown on the thermometer.

0   20   40   60 °C

_____ °C

1 mark

3 Estimate the length of the curved line. Do not measure the line.

_____ cm

1 mark

PS **4** The same parcel is shown
on both sets of scales.
Estimate the mass of
the parcel.   _____ kg

2kg   500g
                      2kg

1 mark

Marks.........../4

Total marks ..../13   How am I doing?   😊   😐   😖

71

Converting Measures

PS Problem-solving questions

Challenge 1

1 Convert these measurements.

Length

a) 30 mm = _____ cm

b) 400 cm = _____ m

c) 5000 m = _____ km

d) 6 cm = _____ mm

e) 5 m = _____ cm

f) 9 km = _____ m

Mass

g) 4000 g = _____ kg

h) 40 000 g = _____ kg

i) 5 kg = _____ g

Capacity

j) 8 litres = _____ ml

k) 10 000 ml = _____ litres

l) 0.5 litres = _____ ml

12 marks

PS **2** A glass holds 500 ml. How many times can the glass be filled from a 2 litre bottle of drink? _____

1 mark

PS **3** Tina is fitting a kitchen cupboard. The cupboard is 600 mm wide and the space for it is 65 cm.

a) Will the cupboard fit in the space? _____

b) What is the difference between the two measurements? _____

2 marks

Marks......... /15

Challenge 2

1 Convert these measurements.

a) 5.2 m = _____ cm

b) $3\frac{1}{2}$ kg = _____ g

c) 3500 ml = _____ litres

d) 78 mm = _____ cm

e) 250 m = _____ km

f) $\frac{3}{4}$ m = _____ cm

g) 845 cm = _____ m

h) 10 500 m = _____ km

8 marks

Converting Measures

 PS **2** Sara buys a bag of flour that weighs 1 kilogram. She uses some flour and there are 600 grams left. How much flour has Sara used?

_____
1 mark

PS **3** Casey has three jugs. Jug A holds 200 ml, jug B holds 250 ml and jug C holds 500 ml. Which jug will he fill exactly four times to fill a bowl with 1 litre of water?

_____
1 mark

PS **4** Ewan has a carton with 568 millilitres of milk. He uses 0.5 litres in a recipe. How much milk does he have left over?

_____
1 mark

Marks......... /11

Challenge 3

1 How many millimetres are there in 1 metre? _____ mm

1 mark

2 Write in the missing units.

a) 4.5 km = 4500 _____

b) 67 mm = 6.7 _____

c) 125 m = 0.125 _____

d) 6750 ml = 6.75 _____

e) 5.4 kg = 5400 _____

f) 4.5 m = 450 _____

6 marks

PS **3** Each row and each column adds up to 1 litre. Fill in the missing capacities.

$\frac{1}{2}$ litre	300 ml	
	0.6 litres	
$\frac{1}{4}$ litre		

1 mark

Marks......... /8

Total marks .... /34   How am I doing?

Measurement Calculations

PS) Problem-solving questions

Challenge 1

PS **1** Charlotte spends £3.45 on a new pen. How much change will she get from £5?

£ _____

1 mark

PS **2** Nadia buys a book for £8.49 and a magazine for £4.75. How much does she spend?

£ _____

1 mark

PS **3** Tomas buys three pens that cost £2 each. How much change will he get from £10?

£ _____

1 mark

PS **4** Subtract 5p from £5.

£ _____

1 mark

PS **5** Milly has a £10 note and a £5 note. She spends £12.33. How much money will Milly have left?

£ _____

1 mark

Marks.......... /5

Challenge 2

1 Calculate these measures.

a)
```
   £ 2 . 4 5
 + £ 4 . 6 5
 _____
```

b)
```
   1 4 . 8 5 m
 - 1 1 . 0 9 m
 _____
```

c)
```
   5 6 . 7 8 kg
 - 3 8 . 5 8 kg
 _____
```

d)
```
   3 8 . 9 5 litres
 +   7 . 8 4 litres
 _____
```

4 marks

PS **2** Claire goes out for a meal. She spends £15.75 on her main course and £5.50 on dessert. She has £15.35 left. How much did Claire have when she went out?

£_____

1 mark

PS **3** Rachael buys two bags of dog food. Each bag weighs 5 kg. Seven days later, she has used 3.5 kg. How much dog food does Rachael have left?

_____ kg

1 mark

Measurement Calculations

PS **4** At a Sports Day, Mahmood makes three jumps of 3.15 m, 2.87 m and 3.08 m. He adds the distances together. He is 0.15 m short of the school record. What is the school record? _____ m

1 mark

PS **5** David buys some bottles of juice for a party. He buys five 2 litre bottles and ten 0.5 litre bottles. How much juice does he have altogether? _____ litres

1 mark

Marks.......... /8

Challenge 3

PS **1** Asel uses some weights to find the mass of a parcel. She uses two 1 kilogram weights, three 500 gram weights and one 50 gram weight. What is the mass of the parcel?

a) Give your answer in kilograms. _____ kg

b) Give your answer in grams. _____ g

2 marks

PS **2** Toby has £7.25 in his money box. He counts the coins; he has these coins. One coin is missing.

What is the missing coin? _____

1 mark

PS **3** Kitchen cupboards come in two sizes of width: 0.6 m and 0.4 m. Norman wants to use both sizes of cupboards to fill a 3 metre wall. How could he do this?

_____

1 mark

PS **4** A glass holds 450 ml. Yanqun has a 2 litre bottle of drink. How many times can Yanqun fill the glass? _____

1 mark

Marks.......... /5

Total marks .... /18   How am I doing? 😊 😐 😣

12 and 24 Hour Time

Challenge 1

1 These clocks show morning times.
Write the times shown on the clocks in 12 hour time.

a) _____ b) _____ c) _____

3 marks

2 These clocks show afternoon and evening times.
Write the times shown on the clocks in 24 hour time.

a) _____ b) _____ c) _____

3 marks

3 Write the time shown on these clocks in words.

a) _____ b) _____ c) _____

_____ _____ _____

3 marks

Marks.........../9

12 and 24 Hour Time

Challenge 2

1 Write these digital times in 12 hour time.

a) 15:25 _____   b) 18:10 _____

2 marks

2 Write these word times in 24 hour time.

a) Quarter past two in the afternoon _____

b) Ten to twelve in the morning _____

c) Twenty-five to seven in the evening _____

3 marks

PS **3** The time on this clock is 40 minutes slow.

What is the correct time? _____

1 mark

Marks.......... /6

Challenge 3

1 Write the missing parts of each time in this table.

	Word time		12 hour time		24 hour time
a)	Five past two in the afternoon	=	_____:05 _____	=	_____:05
b)	Twenty-five to _____ in the evening	=	8:_____ _____	=	_____:_____

2 marks

PS **2** Harpreet's train leaves at 15:25.
She looks at her watch.
How many minutes is it before her
train leaves? _____ minutes

1 mark

Marks.........../3

Total marks .... /18   How am I doing?

77

Time Problems

Challenge 1

1 Write in the missing numbers.

a) 2 minutes = _____ seconds b) 2 hours = _____ minutes

c) 2 days = _____ hours d) 2 weeks = _____ days

4 marks

2 Write the four months of the year that have exactly 30 days.

_____ _____

_____ _____

4 marks

3 If the year 2020 is a leap year, which year will be the next leap year? _____

1 mark

PS **4** Kim's birthday is on Tuesday, 4th May.
She has her birthday party on the first Saturday after her birthday.

What is the date of the birthday party? _____

1 mark

Marks......... /10

Challenge 2

PS **1** A film starts at 16:45 and finishes at 19:05.

How long does it last? _____ hours _____ minutes

1 mark

PS **2** Carly gets up when her alarm clock shows 07:30.
She gets washed and dressed and has her breakfast. Her watch shows the time that she leaves for school.

How long has it taken her to get ready? _____ minutes

1 mark

PS **3** It is 18:30 and Bev says, "I'll see you in three-quarters of an hour."

What will the time be? _____

1 mark

Time Problems

4 Change these units of time.

a) 4 weeks = _____ days   b) 2 years = _____ months

c) 5 minutes = _____ seconds d) 3 days = _____ hours

4 marks

Marks.......... /7

Challenge 3

PS **1** These time periods are in order, shortest first.
Write the number of minutes that could be the missing number.

480 seconds	_____ minutes	$\frac{1}{6}$ of an hour

1 mark

2 Write in the missing numbers.

a) _____ hours = _____ days = 2 weeks

b) _____ months = _____ years = 1 decade

2 marks

PS **3** Barry goes to sleep at 21:30 and he sleeps for $9\frac{1}{4}$ hours.

At what time will he wake up?   _____

1 mark

PS **4** School starts at 8:50am and ends at 12:15pm. The children have a 20-minute break. The rest of the time they are in the classroom.

For how long are they in the classroom?

_____ hours _____ minutes

1 mark

PS **5** Karen catches a train at 10:15am.
The journey lasts 3 hours 12 minutes.

At what time does the train arrive? _____

1 mark

Marks.......... /6

Total marks .... /23   How am I doing?

Perimeter and Area

Challenge 1

1 Three rectangles and squares (**A–C**) are drawn on a centimetre square grid. Find **a)** the area and **b)** the perimeter of each shape.

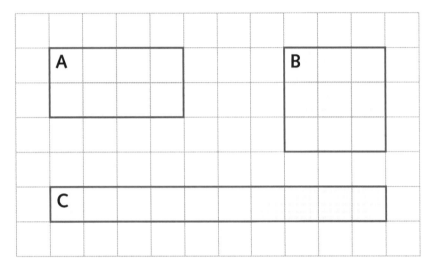

A   a) _____ squares

    b) _____ cm

B   a) _____ squares

    b) _____ cm

C   a) _____ squares

    b) _____ cm

6 marks

Grid not to scale

Marks.......... /6

Challenge 2

1 Three shapes (**A–C**) are drawn on a centimetre square grid. Find **a)** the area and **b)** the perimeter of each shape.

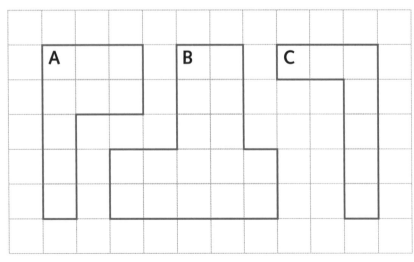

A   a) _____ squares

    b) _____ cm

B   a) _____ squares

    b) _____ cm

C   a) _____ squares

    b) _____ cm

6 marks

Grid not to scale

Perimeter and Area

2   Work out the perimeter of this shape. Use a ruler. _____ cm

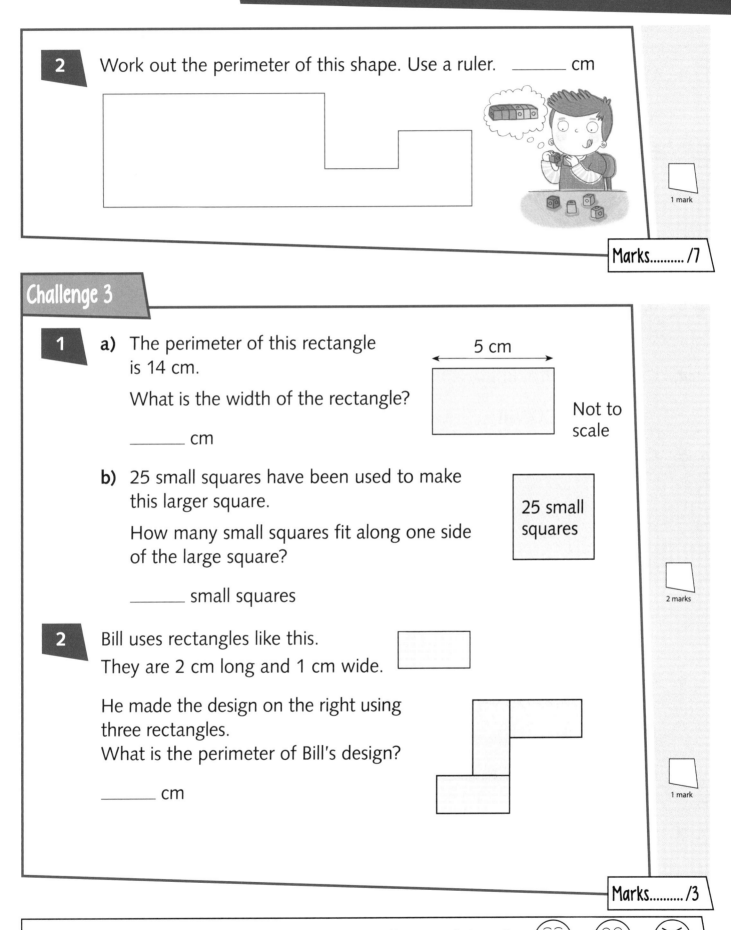

1 mark

Marks.........../7

Challenge 3

1   **a)**   The perimeter of this rectangle is 14 cm.

What is the width of the rectangle?

5 cm

Not to scale

_____ cm

b)   25 small squares have been used to make this larger square.

How many small squares fit along one side of the large square?

25 small squares

_____ small squares

2 marks

2   Bill uses rectangles like this.
They are 2 cm long and 1 cm wide.

He made the design on the right using three rectangles.
What is the perimeter of Bill's design?

_____ cm

1 mark

Marks.........../3

Total marks ..../16   How am I doing? 😊   😐   😖

Progress Test 3

1. Write in the missing numbers.

   a) 63 _____ 81 _____ 99 108

   b) 36 _____ _____ 54 60 66

   2 marks

2. Write these numbers in order, largest first.

   3572　　　3752　　　3725　　　3727　　　3527

   _____ _____ _____ _____ _____

   1 mark

PS 3. Write a four-digit number with 8 ones,
   5 hundreds, 6 thousands and 4 tens. _____

   1 mark

4. Circle the Roman numeral that is the largest number.

   XXVIII　　　LXV　　　XL　　　XXXIX

   1 mark

5. Complete the table by rounding these numbers to the nearest 100.

Number	Rounded to the nearest hundred
7 8 2 3	
7 8 2	
7 8	

   3 marks

PS 6. Each day a school kitchen prepares 240 hot meals,
   180 salads and 125 vegetarian meals.

   a) How many meals are prepared each day? _____

   b) On Monday, 43 meals are left uneaten.
   How many meals are eaten on Monday? _____

   2 marks

7. Write in the missing numbers.

   a) $6 \times$ _____ $= 36$　　　b) $48 \div$ _____ $= 8$

   c) _____ $\times 9 = 45$　　　d) _____ $\div 7 = 7$

   4 marks

8. Fill in the missing number. $6 \times 5 \times$ _____ $= 240$

1 mark

9. Work out:

a)   5   0   9   b)   4   5   2   c)   8   6   1

$\times$ 9 $\times$ 7 $\times$ 6

_____   _____   _____

_____   _____   _____

3 marks

PS **10.** It takes Alice 2 hours to build 7 metres of fence.
How long will it take her to build 21 metres of fence?   _____ hours

1 mark

11. Write in the missing numbers.

a) $6 \div$ _____ $= \frac{6}{100}$ b) $8.1 \div$ _____ $= \frac{81}{100}$

c) $0.7 \div$ _____ $= \frac{7}{100}$

3 marks

12. Draw a line from $\frac{3}{5}$ to its equivalent fraction.

$\frac{4}{8}$

$\frac{4}{6}$

$\frac{3}{5}$

$\frac{6}{10}$

$\frac{1}{2}$

1 mark

13. Fill in the missing numbers.

a) $\frac{\square}{8} + \frac{6}{8} = \frac{7}{8}$

b) $\frac{\square}{12} + \frac{5}{12} + \frac{3}{12} = \frac{11}{12}$

2 marks

PS **14.** Heather has saved up £18.70.
Write this to the nearest whole pound.   £ _____

1 mark

PS **15.** Mo has £20.

She spends $\frac{1}{5}$ of her money on a drink and $\frac{3}{10}$ on a sandwich.
How much money does she have left?   £ _____

1 mark

Progress Test 3

PS ⟩ **16.** Kate buys some things for her party.

| Balloons £1.75 | Candles £3.85 | Cake £11.85 | Plates £5.80 | Mugs £4.80 |

a) She spends exactly £17.45. Which three things did she buy?

_____ _____ _____

b) Kate pays with a £20 note.
How much money does she have left?   £ _____

2 marks

17. Write these amounts in order, starting with the largest.

£3   90p   £0.08   £1.25   5p

_____ _____ _____ _____ _____

1 mark

PS ⟩ **18.** Harvey spends £8, Tia spends 675p, Christopher spends £9.89 and Raf spends two £5 notes.

a) Who spends the least?   _____

b) Who spends the most?   _____

2 marks

PS ⟩ **19.** Daryl estimates how much money he has spent. He paid £17.45 for a ticket to a theme park, £8.40 for food and £15.35 on gifts.

He rounds each amount to the nearest whole pound and adds the rounded amounts.

Write Daryl's estimate.   £ _____

1 mark

PS ⟩ **20.** Katherine says, "My train leaves at quarter to 9."
The clock in the station shows 08:30.

How many minutes does Katherine need to wait?   _____ minutes

1 mark

21. The clock on the right shows an evening time.
Circle the digital clock that shows the same time.

A 20:40   B 19:40   C 21:35   D 20:50

1 mark

84

22. Tick the correct statement.

    A   There are 300 minutes in 5 hours. ☐

    B   There are 60 minutes in 5 hours. ☐

    C   There are 35 minutes in 5 hours. ☐

    D   There are 120 minutes in 5 hours. ☐

1 mark

PS **23.** Susie runs a lap of a track in 100 seconds.

Write this as minutes and seconds. _____ minutes _____ seconds

1 mark

24. Change these measurements.

    a) 5 kg = _____ g   **b)** 60 mm = _____ cm

    c) 1000 cm = _____ m   **d)** 8000 ml = _____ litres

    e) 8 m = _____ cm   **f)** 2 km = _____ m

6 marks

25. Measure the perimeter of each shape.

    a)   **b)**

          _____ cm   _____ cm

2 marks

26. Write the area of the shaded shape.   _____ squares

1 mark

Marks........ /46

85

2-D Shapes

Challenge 1

1 Tick the shapes that are rectangles.

A B C D

2 marks

2 These triangles are drawn on a squared grid.

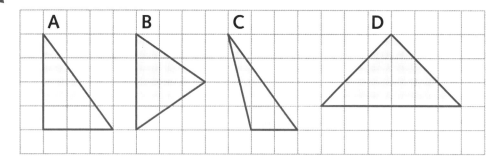

a) Write the letters of the two isosceles triangles. _____ _____

b) Write the letters of the two right-angled triangles. _____ _____

c) Write the letter of the obtuse-angled triangle. _____

d) Write the letter of the acute-angled triangle. _____

4 marks

3 Tick the shape that is a parallelogram.

A B C D

1 mark

Marks.......... /7

Challenge 2

1 Tick the quadrilaterals that are squares.

A B C D

2 marks

2-D Shapes

2 Give a reason why this shape is not a hexagon.

_____

_____

1 mark

3 These triangles are drawn on a squared grid.
Tick the triangle that is a right-angled isosceles triangle.

A   B   C   D

1 mark

Marks.......... /4

Challenge 3

1 Circle the shape that has the most sides.

pentagon   hexagon   parallelogram   octagon

1 mark

2 Tick the shapes with pairs of equal and parallel sides.

A   B   C   D

3 marks

3 Mark says, "A pentagon cannot have a right angle."
Draw a pentagon to show that Mark is incorrect.

1 mark

Marks.......... /5

Total marks .... /16   How am I doing?

3-D Shapes

PS Problem-solving questions

Challenge 1

1 Tick the cube.

A   B   C   D

1 mark

2 Tick the cone.

A   B   C   D

1 mark

3 How many faces does each of these shapes have?

a) _____   b) A cube _____

2 marks

Marks.......... /4

Challenge 2

1 How many faces does each of these shapes have?

a) _____   b) _____

2 marks

2 Tick the correct statement.

A Cuboids do not have faces that are perpendicular and parallel. ☐

B Cuboids only have faces that are perpendicular, and not parallel. ☐

C Cuboids only have faces that are parallel, and not perpendicular. ☐

D Cuboids have faces that are perpendicular and parallel. ☐

1 mark

3 Complete this table.

Shape	Faces	Edges	Vertices
Cuboid			
Square-based pyramid			
Triangular prism			

3 marks

Marks.......... /6

Challenge 3

PS **1** Shona says, "The faces on a cuboid are always rectangles."
Is Shona correct? Explain your answer.

_____

_____

_____

1 mark

2 A prism has 15 edges. What shape is its end face?

_____

1 mark

3 **a)** How many cubes have been used to make this shape? _____

b) Rohan adds more cubes to this shape to make a cuboid. The cuboid is 3 cubes long, 2 cubes wide and 2 cubes high.

How many more cubes will Rohan need? _____

2 marks

Marks.......... /4

Total marks .... /14   How am I doing?

Lines of Symmetry

Challenge 1

1 Draw the lines of symmetry on these shapes.

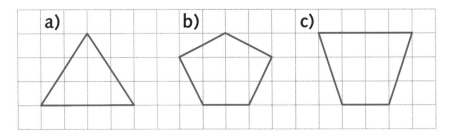

a)   b)   c)

3 marks

2 The dotted lines are lines of symmetry. Complete the shapes.

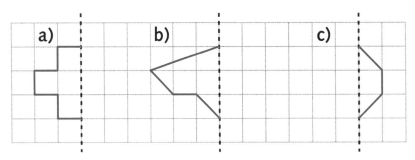

a)   b)   c)

3 marks

Marks.......... /6

Challenge 2

1 How many lines of symmetry does each of these shapes have?

a)

_____

b)

_____

c)

_____

3 marks

Lines of Symmetry

2 The dotted lines are lines of symmetry. Complete the shapes.

2 marks

Marks.......... /5

1 Tick the shape that has no lines of symmetry.

A   B   C   D   E

1 mark

2 Draw three more lines on the grid to make a pentagon with one line of symmetry.

1 mark

Marks.......... /2

Total marks .... /13   How am I doing?

Angles

Challenge 1

1 Write the number of angles in each shape.

a) Rectangle   b) Hexagon   c) Kite

_____   _____   _____

3 marks

2 Tick the acute angle.

A   B   C   D

1 mark

3 Tick the obtuse angle.

A   B   C   D

1 mark

4 Tick the largest angle.

A   B   C   D

1 mark

Marks.......... /6

Challenge 2

1 Here are two shapes drawn on a squared grid.
Tick the acute angles in each shape.

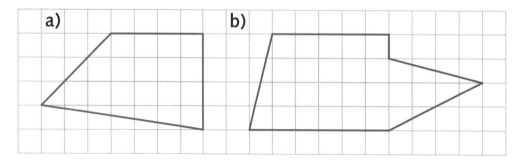

a)   b)

2 marks

Angles

2 Write the letters of these angles in order of size, smallest first.

A   B   C   D

_____   _____   _____   _____

1 mark

3 Write these angles in order of size, starting with the largest.

right   obtuse   acute

_____   _____   _____

1 mark

Marks.......... /4

Challenge 3

Below is a squared grid.

a) Draw a five-sided shape with three obtuse angles.

b) Draw a four-sided shape with three acute angles.

2 marks

PS

Caroline says, "Any 2-D shape can have two right angles."
Is Caroline correct? Give a reason for your answer.

_____

_____

1 mark

Marks.......... /3

Total marks .... /13   How am I doing?   :)   :| >:(

Translations

Challenge 1

1 A square is drawn in different positions on a grid.

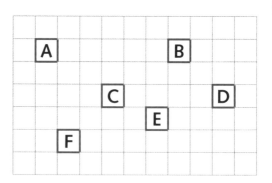

Listed below are translations of the squares. Write the letter of the position the square moves to.

a) Square A moves 3 right and 2 down. _____

b) Square F moves 7 right and 2 up. _____

c) Square B moves 5 left and 4 down. _____

d) Square E moves 5 left and 3 up. _____

e) Square C moves 3 right and 2 up. _____

f) Write the letters of the squares that show the translation

2 right and 2 down. Square _____ to square _____.

6 marks

Marks.......... /6

Challenge 2

1 A rectangle is drawn in different positions on a grid.

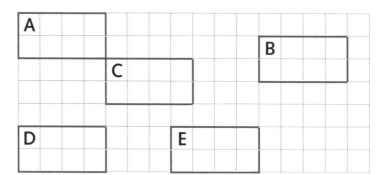

Describe these translations of the rectangle.

a) From A to B _____

Translations

b) From E to C _____

c) From B to C _____

d) From D to B _____

e) From A to C _____

f) From C to D _____

6 marks

Marks.......... /6

Challenge 3

1 A triangle is translated 5 units left and 7 units down.
Write the translation that moves the triangle to its original position.

_____

1 mark

2 Here is a square drawn on a grid.

a) Translate the square 4 right and
2 up. Draw the square.

b) Translate the square 1 left and
1 up. Draw the square.

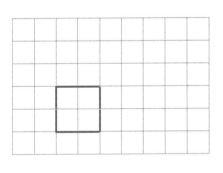

2 marks

3 Circle the correct bold word in each statement.

a) A triangle is translated 6 units left and 0 units down.

This will leave the triangle in the same **row / column**.

b) A rectangle is translated 0 units right and 5 units up.

This will leave the rectangle in the
same **row / column**.

2 marks

Marks.......... /5

Total marks .... /17   How am I doing?

Coordinates

Challenge 1

1 Look at the coordinate grid. Write the coordinates of these symbols.

a) ★ _____   b) ♥ _____

c) ⚡ _____   d) ✚ _____

e) ♠ _____   f) ☾ _____

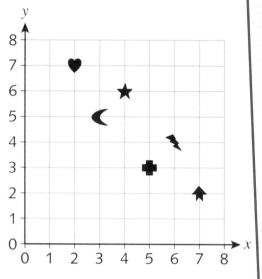

6 marks

2 Look again at the coordinate grid.

a) Plot these points on the grid: (1, 2) and (7, 8).

Join the points with a straight line.

b) What are the coordinates of the mid-point of the line? _____

2 marks

Marks.......... /8

Challenge 2

1 Plot these points on the grid. Show each point by writing the capital letter.

a) A (6,1)   b) B (5,7)

c) C (2,6)   d) D (7,4)

e) E (1,3)   f) F (4,2)

6 marks

Coordinates

2 **a)** A point is plotted at (6,4). It is then moved 1 unit left and 1 unit down.

What are the new coordinates of the point?   _____

b) A point is plotted at (2,1). It is then moved 3 units right and 2 units up.

What are the new coordinates of the point?   _____

2 marks

Marks.......... /8

Challenge 3

1 There are some mystery coordinates.
Work out the coordinates, write them on the lines and plot them on the coordinate grid.

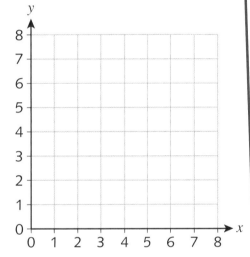

a) The x-coordinate and the y-coordinate add up to 9.
The cordinates are both multiples of 3.
The x-coordinate is the larger number.   _____

b) The x-coordinate and the y-coordinate add up to 10.
The x-coordinate is 4 greater than the y-coordinate.   _____

c) The difference between the coordinates is 2.
The y-coordinate is double the x-coordinate.   _____

d) The x-coordinate + the y-coordinate = 13.
The x-coordinate − the y-coordinate = 1.   _____

8 marks

Marks.......... /8

Total marks .... /24   How am I doing?

Shapes and Coordinates

Challenge 1

1 **a)** Plot these points on the coordinate grid: (1,7) (1,4) (6,7). They are three vertices of a rectangle.

b) Plot the fourth vertex and use a ruler to complete the rectangle.

c) Write the coordinates of the fourth vertex. _____

3 marks

2 **a)** Plot these points on the coordinate grid: (7,3) (3,1). They are two vertices of a right-angled triangle.

b) Plot the third vertex and use a ruler to complete the triangle.

c) Write the coordinates of the third vertex. _____

3 marks

Marks.......... /6

Challenge 2

1 **a)** Plot these points on the coordinate grid: (3,8) (1,6) (5,6). They are three vertices of a square.

b) Plot the fourth vertex and use a ruler to complete the square.

c) Write the coordinates of the fourth vertex. _____

3 marks

2 **a)** Plot these points on the coordinate grid: (6,6) (4,4) (8,4). They are three vertices of a kite.

b) Plot a possible fourth vertex. Use a ruler to complete the kite.

c) Write possible coordinates of the fourth vertex. _____

3 marks

Marks.......... /6

Shapes and Coordinates

Challenge 3

 1 Three vertices of a square are: (10,15) (10,10) (15,15).

Write the coordinates of the fourth vertex. _____

1 mark

 2 Matt draws a straight line on a coordinate grid.
He uses these coordinates:
(1,5) (3,6) (5,7) (7,8).
Matt extends the line.

Write the next pair of coordinates
in the sequence. _____

1 mark

3 a) These coordinates are the end points of a line: (2,2) (8,8).

Write the mid-point of the line. _____

b) These coordinates are the end points of a line: (2,8) (8,2).

Write the mid-point of the line. _____

2 marks

4 Daria says, "If there is a set of coordinates and the first number is always the same, that means the line joining them must be a horizontal line."

Is Daria correct? Explain your answer.

_____

_____

_____

_____

1 mark

Marks.......... /5

Total marks .... /17   How am I doing?

Bar Charts

Look at the bar chart below to answer the questions on pages 100 and 101.
It shows the points scored by five teams on school sports day.

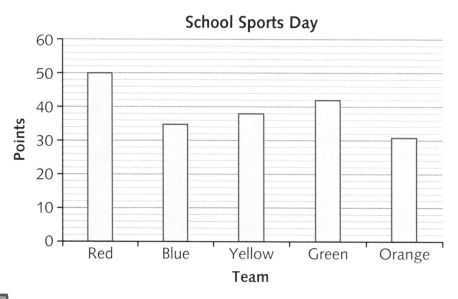

School Sports Day

Challenge 1

PS **1** a) What is each small division on the
vertical axis worth? _____

b) Which team scored the most number
of points? _____

c) Which team scored the least number
of points? _____

d) Which team scored 35 points? _____

e) How many more points did the Red
team score than the Blue team? _____

5 marks

Marks.........../5

Challenge 2

PS **1** a) How many teams scored more than 35 points? _____

b) Circle the score for the Yellow team.

Bar Charts

c) What was the Green team's score? _____

d) What was the difference in the scores between the Blue and Orange teams? _____

e) What was the difference in the scores between the Yellow and Green teams? _____

5 marks

Marks.......... /5

Challenge 3

 1 On sports day, 1st place gained 8 points, 2nd place gained 5 points and 3rd place gained 2 points.

a) What was the points difference between the highest scoring and lowest scoring teams? _____

b) How many points were awarded in total? _____

c) The Green team won three races. Explain how they won the other points.

_____

_____

d) Simon says, "The Red team won Sports Day, but never won a race."

Could Simon be correct? Explain your answer.

_____

_____

_____

_____

4 marks

Marks.......... /4

Total marks .... /14   How am I doing?

Time Graphs

PS Problem-solving questions

A class recorded the temperature in the playground throughout one day.
Look at their time graph below to answer the questions on pages 102 and 103.

Playground Temperature

Challenge 1

PS 1 **a)** Write the time the temperature was first taken.

_____

b) Write the highest temperature. _____°C

c) Write the temperature at 3:00pm. _____°C

d) For how many hours did the class record the temperature?

_____

e) By how many degrees did the temperature rise between 9:00am and 11:00am?

_____°C

5 marks

Marks.........../5

Time Graphs

Challenge 2

 1

a) At what time did the temperature first start to go down? _____

b) From the first recording, how long did it take for the temperature to reach 8°C? _____

c) For how long did the temperature stay at 7°C? _____

d) Estimate the temperature at 10:00am. _____°C

e) Estimate the time the temperature first reached 6°C. _____

5 marks

Marks.......... /5

Challenge 3

 1

a) What is the difference between the temperature at 9:00am and 4:00pm? _____°C

b) What was the temperature at 12:30pm? _____°C

c) Estimate the temperature at 9:30am. _____°C

d) Estimate the time the temperature was above 6°C. _____

e) Estimate the time it took for the temperature to fall from 8°C to 4°C. _____

5 marks

Marks.......... /5

Total marks .... /15   How am I doing?

Pictograms

PS Problem-solving questions

Challenge 1

PS **1** This pictogram shows the number of rainy days from January to March in four cities.

City	Rainy days
Carlisle	
Birmingham	
Manchester	
Norwich	

represents 4 rainy days

a) How many rainy days are represented by a rainy cloud symbol? _____

b) How many rainy days were there in Carlisle? _____

c) How many more rainy days were there in Manchester than in Birmingham? _____

d) How many fewer rainy days were there in Carlisle than in Manchester? _____

e) The pictogram is not finished. There were 20 rainy days in Norwich. How many rainy day symbols will complete the pictogram for Norwich? _____

5 marks

Marks.......... /5

Challenge 2

PS **1** This pictogram shows the number of kilometres five friends cycled in one week.

represents 10 kilometres

Name	Number of kilometres
Sami	
Greg	
Ava	
Martha	
Ricardo	

Pictograms

a) Which two friends cycled the same distance?

_____ and _____

b) How far did Martha cycle? _____ km

c) How much further did Sami cycle than Ricardo? _____ km

d) How many friends cycled more than 80 km? _____

4 marks

Marks.......... /4

Challenge 3

PS 1 This pictogram shows the number of rooms in different hotels.

	🛏 represents 20 rooms
Hotel	**Number of rooms**
Mill Hotel	🛏 🛏 🛏 🛏 🛏 🛏 🛏
Riverbank	🛏 🛏 🛏 🛏
Bridge Hotel	🛏 🛏 🛏 🛏 🛏
Valley Hotel	🛏 🛏 🛏
Old Barn	🛏 🛏

a) How many more rooms are there at the
Bridge Hotel than at the Old Barn? _____

b) How many rooms are there at the Old
Barn and the Valley Hotel together? _____

c) The Riverbank is only half full.
How many rooms are taken? _____

d) 20 rooms at the Mill Hotel are empty.
How many rooms are taken? _____

4 marks

Marks.......... /4

Total marks .... /13   How am I doing?

105

Tables

PS Problem-solving questions

Challenge 1

PS 1 This table shows the prices of some shirts.

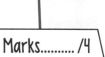

Size Design	Small	Medium	Large
Short-sleeved	£12	£14	£16
Long-sleeved	£15	£18	£21

a) What is the cost of a medium long-sleeved shirt? £ _____

b) What is the cost of 2 short-sleeved large shirts? £ _____

c) How much more expensive is a large long-sleeved shirt than a medium short-sleeved shirt? £ _____

d) Gordon buys a small short-sleeved shirt and a small long-sleeved shirt.
How much will he have left from £40? £ _____

4 marks

Marks.......... /4

Challenge 2

PS 1 This table shows the dinner choices of children in different classes.

Class Meal	A	B	C	Total
Hot meal	18	17	12	_____
Vegetarian meal	5	4	_____	18
Sandwich	_____	8	7	20
Total	28	29	28	85

a) How many more children had a hot meal than a vegetarian meal or a sandwich in Class B? _____

Tables

---

b) How many children had a hot meal altogether?
Add this to the table.

c) The number of children who had a sandwich in Class A is missing. Calculate the missing number and add it to the table.

d) The number of children who had a vegetarian meal in Class C is missing. Calculate the missing number and add it to the table.

4 marks

Marks.......... /4

Challenge 3

PS   **1**   This table gives information about visitors to a castle.

Visitor \ Day	Friday	Saturday	Sunday	Total
Men	24	18	6	48
Women	_____	38	12	76
Children	_____	_____	16	_____
Total	55	71	34	160

a) How many more men and women visited on Saturday than on Sunday? _____

b) Olivia says, "As many men visited on Friday as on Saturday and Sunday together." Is Olivia correct? Explain how you know.

_____

_____

c) How many children visited on Friday? _____

d) Which was the largest group of visitors: men, women or children? _____

4 marks

Marks.......... /4

Total marks .... /12   How am I doing?

Progress Test 4

1. Write these numbers in order, starting with the smallest.

   9018   9801   9810   9108   9180

   _____   _____   _____   _____   _____

   1 mark

2. Write the value of the 4 in each number.

   a) 7451 _____   b) 4925 _____   c) 745 _____

   3 marks

3. Write the number of tens altogether in 560. _____

   1 mark

PS 4. Write in the missing numbers.

   a)
   $$
   \begin{array}{ccccc}
    & 7 & 5 & \square & \square \\
   + & \square & \square & 1 & 2 \\
   \hline
    & 9 & 3 & 1 & 5 \\
   \hline
   \end{array}
   $$

   b)
   $$
   \begin{array}{cccc}
    & 8 & \square & \square \\
   - & \square & 6 & 2 \\
   \hline
    & 4 & 9 & 2 \\
   \hline
   \end{array}
   $$

   2 marks

PS 5. Kerry buys some trays of plants for her garden. She buys 14 trays with 4 plants and 15 trays with 6 plants.

   How many plants does she buy altogether? _____ plants

   1 mark

PS 6. A pizza is cut into twelfths. Jonah eats $\frac{3}{12}$ and Ken eats $\frac{4}{12}$.

   How many twelfths are left? _____

   1 mark

PS 7. Larry uses $\frac{1}{5}$ of 5 kg of potatoes on Saturday

   and $\frac{1}{2}$ of what is left on Sunday.

   How many kilograms are left? _____ kg

   1 mark

8. Write these weights in order, starting with the smallest.

   5500 g $4\frac{1}{2}$ kg   4.9 kg   5 kg   4100 g

   _____   _____   _____   _____   _____

   1 mark

PS 9. Laura spends three weeks of her summer holiday staying with her grandmother.

   How many days is this? _____ days

   1 mark

10. Draw lines to match each clock to the equivalent digital clock.

a)   b)   c)

1 mark

11. Convert these measures.

a) 8000 g = _____ kg   b) 9 litres = _____ ml

c) 500 mm = _____ cm   d) 4.5 m = _____ cm

4 marks

PS **12.** Cai has two jugs that each hold 2.25 litres and a third jug that holds 3.75 litres.

How much can the three jugs hold altogether? _____ litres

1 mark

13. Work out:

a) 5 kg – 500 g = _____   b) 5 m – 500 cm = _____

2 marks

14. Below is a triangle. Circle two words, one from each column, to describe the triangle.

acute-angled   scalene

right-angled   isosceles

obtuse-angled   equilateral

2 marks

15. Write the number of lines of symmetry in each shape.

a)   b)

_____ lines of symmetry   _____ lines of symmetry

2 marks

PS ⟩ Problem-solving questions

16. What type of angle is this?

_____

1 mark

17. A square is translated from position A to position B. Complete the sentence:

The square has moved _____ square(s)

to the left and _____ square(s) up.

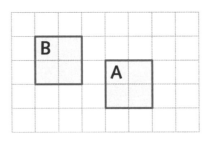

1 mark

18. Look at the coordinate grid.

a) Write the letter at the coordinates (3,6).   _____

b) Carl joins the points A, B, C and D to make a straight line. He makes the line longer; write the coordinates of a point on the line.

(_____ , _____)

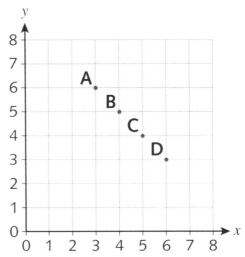

2 marks

PS **19.** This table shows the number of drinks sold in a café one weekend.

Day \ Drink	Teas	Coffees	Milkshakes	Juice	Total
Saturday	45	75	12	23	_____
Sunday	38	62	_____	35	150
Total	83	_____	_____	58	305

a) How many drinks were sold on Saturday?   _____ drinks

b) How many coffees were sold altogether?   _____ coffees

c) How many milkshakes were sold on Sunday?   _____ milkshakes

3 marks

PS **20.** This time graph shows the rainfall over one week.

a) What was the greatest amount of rainfall recorded that week? _____ mm

b) Which days had no rain? _____ and _____

c) On how many days was there over 5 mm of rain? _____ days

3 marks

PS **21.** This bar chart shows the marks of five children in a test.

a) Write the name of the person who scored 15. _____

b) Write how many more marks Nia scored than Liz. _____

2 marks

Marks........ /36

Notes

For questions worth one mark with several answer spaces, all answers should be correct to achieve the mark, unless otherwise indicated.

Pages 4–11
Starter Test
1. a) 32, 36   b) 550, 600
2. 760
3. a) <   b) <
4. 871 circled
5. a) 25   b) 70
6. a) 821   b) 576   c) 358
7. 252
8. 635
9. a) 443   b) 384
10. 693 – 265
11. a) 54   b) 96   c) 112
12. a) 14   b) 19   c) 18
13. 72
14. 23
15. 48p
16. a) $\frac{1}{2}$ (accept equivalent fractions)
   b) $\frac{7}{8}$
17. $\frac{1}{10}$
18. a) 4   b) 16   c) $\frac{4}{5}$
19. a) $\frac{2}{5}$ (accept $\frac{4}{10}$ or 0.4)
   b) $\frac{9}{10}$ (accept 0.9)
20. a) $\frac{2}{6}$ b) $\frac{4}{8}$
21. a) <   b) >
22. a) $\frac{2}{5}$ b) $\frac{3}{10}$ c) $\frac{7}{8}$
23. one
24. $\frac{7}{8}$
25. 1 mm, 1 cm, 1 m
26. 2 m circled
27. a) >   b) >
28. 0.5 kg ticked
29. a) >   b) >
30. 4 litres
31. 3 kg (accept any weight ≥2.8 kg but ≤3.2 kg)
32. a) 400 ml (accept any capacity ≥380 ml but ≤420 ml)
   b) 250 ml (accept any capacity ≥230 ml but ≤270 ml)
33. a) 2:20pm   b) 9:50am
   c) 8:30am   d) 9:45pm
34. a) 9:15pm   b) 6:55am
35. 180 seconds
36. 30th September circled
37. 365 days
38. 50 minutes
39. 16 cm
40. £12.30
41. £89.85
42. a) 800 cm   b) 11 kg
   c) 2 litres   d) 45 mm
43. Line **B** ticked
44. Lines circled in Hexagon **C**
45. A pentagon with one right angle drawn
46. a) cuboid   b) cone   c) 6
   d) circle
47. Angles **A** and **C** ticked
48. 2
49. a) 55   b) 64
50. a) Ben   b) 3   c) 5
   d) Bar for Gus, representing 5 lengths, added to chart
51. a) 8   b) 4   c) 6

Pages 12–13
Challenge 1
1. a) 40, 48   b) 48, 54
2. a) Add 6   b) Add 25
3. No
4. 56
Challenge 2
1. a) 42, 48   b) 200, 225
2. a) Add 7   b) Add 25
3. 650
Challenge 3
1. 135, 144, 153
2. 60, 66, 72
3. 71
4.

Add 7 →				
21	28	35	42	49
30	37	44	**51**	58
39	**46**	53	60	67
48	55	62	69	76

(Add 9 ↓)

Pages 14–15
Challenge 1
1. a) <   b) >   c) <
2. Statement **C** ticked
3. 3465, 3563, 4536, 4645, 4654
4. 7541
Challenge 2
1. a) >   b) <   c) <
2. 4138, 4831, 5246, 5264, 5642
3. a) 865   b) 1356

Answers

Challenge 3
1. 681, 5891, 7861, 11 937, 12 612
2. Any number >6285 but <6290
3. Athletic vs Wanderers

Pages 16–17
Challenge 1
1. a) 40   b) 400   c) 4
2. 1475 circled
3. 341 circled
4. 3627
Challenge 2
1. a) 900   b) 90   c) 9000
2. 3890
3. 9738
4. 6342
5. a) Any combination of four digits with 5 or 6 as the first digit.
   b) 2345
Challenge 3
1. Jamie is incorrect because 4021 has four digits (thousands), which is more than 897 which only has three digits (hundreds).
2. 6031
3. a) 10 009   b) 10 090

Pages 18–19
Challenge 1
1. a) 12   b) 15   c) 26
   d) 8   e) 33   f) 40
2. a) $3 + 2 = 5$ b) $6 + 4 = 10$
   c) $26 - 7 = 19$
3. a) 4:40 **or** twenty to five
   b) 10:20 **or** twenty past ten
Challenge 2
1. a) 56   b) 48   c) 96   d) 83
2. 90
3. a) $40 + 60 = 100$ b) $69 - 30 = 39$
4. XCIX circled
Challenge 3
1. XXXVIII, XLVII, LXV, LXIX, XC
2. a) 46   b) 136   c) 50   d) 84
3. a) 125   b) 222   c) 359

Pages 20–21
Challenge 1
1. a) 200   b) 400
   c) Any number >420 but <480
2. a) 351   b) 524
3. a) 5296   b) 7570   c) 2804
Challenge 2
1. 457
2. a) 4000 + 800 + 20 + 5 (accept alternatives such as 3000 + 1800 + 20 + 5)

b) 6000 + 700 + 10 + 9 (accept alternatives such as 3000 + 3700 + 10 + 9)
3. a) Any number >3450 but <3550
   b) Any number >4100 but <4400
   c) Any number >4600 but <4750
Challenge 3
1. a)–e) Accept any five different additions that total 3746
2. a) 4609   b) 8020
3. a) 7 thousands = **70** hundreds = **700** tens = **7000** ones
   b) 800   c) 3000
4. 2738

Pages 22–23
Challenge 1
1. a) 50   b) 100   c) 80
2. 84, 75 and 77 circled
3. 120
4. a) 300   b) 700   c) 1500
Challenge 2
1. a) 3800   b) 6300   c) 5100
2. a) 2630   b) 2600   c) 3000
3. a) 4000   b) 3000   c) 8000
4. Any three numbers ≥650 but <750
Challenge 3
1. a) 6000   b) 1000   c) 4000
2. Any number ≥7335 but <7345
3. 350, 6000 and 7900 circled
4. 6951, 6915, 6591, 6519

Pages 24–25
Challenge 1
1. a) −2   b) −4   c) −2   d) −5
2. a) −2   b) −4   c) −1
3. £4
4. −5
Challenge 2
1. a) −4   b) −7   c) −2   d) −9
2. a) −5   b) −5   c) −1
3. a) −9   b) −17   c) −18
4. a) −2°C   b) −9°C   c) 4°C
Challenge 3
1. 5, 3, −1, −4, −6
2. a) −6   b) −4   c) 0   d) 4
3. a) −9   b) −15   c) −8
   d) −14   e) −24   f) −4

Pages 26–27
Challenge 1
1. a) 749   b) 997   c) 1005
2. a) 401   b) 91   c) 528

Challenge 2
1. a) 1528   b) 1418   c) 13 728
2. a) 643   b) 406   c) 3596
Challenge 3
1. a) 12 400   b) 11 312   c) 12 909
2. a) 1196   b) 3973   c) 4793

Pages 28–29
Challenge 1
1. a) 120   b) 90   c) 170
2. 390 – 265 circled
3. a) 563 – 328 **or** 563 – 235
    b) 293 + 236   c) 311 + 214
4. 227
Challenge 2
1. 356
2. 630
3. a) 1000   b) 100
4. a) 3000   b) 11 000
Challenge 3
1. Possible answers are: 84p + 51p, 83p + 52p,
    82p + 53p, 81p + 54p
2. a) 17 000   b) 5000
3. 9258 – 3826 = 5432
    Correct answer = 10 258
4. 347

Pages 30–31
Challenge 1
1. a) 147   b) 425
2. 613
3. £54
4. 125 cm
Challenge 2
1. 6797
2. 3303
3. 2093 km
4. 2181
Challenge 3
1. a) 3874 + 2643   b) 8374 – 2650
2. Accept different possible answers: 5 and 3 are
    hundreds, 1 and 2 are tens, and 6 and 4 are
    ones, e.g. 526 + 314
3. A   5236 + 1609 = **6845**
    B   9343 – 2434 = **6909**
    C   2354 + 4567 = **6921** circled
    **(1 mark for each calculation worked out
    correctly; 1 mark for circling calculation C)**

Pages 32–33
Challenge 1
1. a) 35   b) 24   c) 88
    d) 36   e) 70   f) 32

2. a) 7   b) 12   c) 7
    d) 6   e) 10   f) 6
3. a) 8   b) 9   c) 9
    d) 7   e) 6   f) 12
Challenge 2
1. a) 42   b) 28   c) 99
    d) 56   e) 81   f) 84
2. a) 7   b) 8   c) 12
    d) 12   e) 12   f) 9
3. a) 11   b) 3   c) 11
    d) 12   e) 6   f) 4
Challenge 3
1. a)

×	7	9	12
7	49	**63**	**84**
9	**63**	**81**	**108**
12	**84**	**108**	**144**

b)

×	7	8	9
6	42	**48**	**54**
8	**56**	64	**72**
12	84	**96**	108

(1 mark for each correct row)
2. a) Possible answers are: 48 × 1, 24 × 2,
        16 × 3, 12 × 4
    b) Possible answers are: 36 × 1, 18 × 2,
        12 × 3, 6 × 6
    c) Possible answers are: 24 × 1, 12 × 2, 6 × 4
    d) Possible answers are: 72 × 1, 36 × 2,
        24 × 3, 18 × 4, 9 × 8
3. a) 81   b) 56   c) 64   d) 120

Pages 34–35
Challenge 1
1. a) 5   b) 0   c) 0
    d) 60   e) 160   f) 350
2. a) 20   b) 20   c) 30
3. a) 40   b) 30   c) 50
4. a) 3   b) 5   c) 4
Challenge 2
1. a) 30   b) 110   c) 64
    d) 69   e) 128   f) 255
2. a) 15   b) 13   c) 14
    d) 34   e) 16   f) 22
3. a) 48   b) 90   c) 72

Answers

Challenge 3
1. a) 3   b) 4   c) 5
   d) 3   e) 5   f) 3
2. a) 3   b) 6   c) 4
   d) 4   e) 12   f) 3
3. a) 4   b) 3   c) 15   d) 24

Pages 36–37
Challenge 1
1. A, D and F circled
2. a) 5   b) 12
3. 9
4. 1, 3, 5, 10 and 15 circled
Challenge 2
1. a) 1, 2, 5, 10
   b) 1, 3, 7, 21
   c) 1, 2, 4, 8, 16, 32
   d) 1, 2, 4, 5, 8, 10, 20, 40
2. 2 and 21
3. 7 and 8
4. Statement B circled
5. 7
Challenge 3
1.

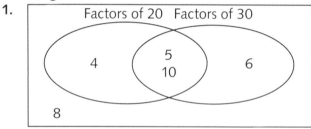

2. 6 rows of 8 bottles
3. a) 48 × 1, 24 × 2, 16 × 3, 12 × 4, 8 × 6
   b) 60 × 1, 30 × 2, 20 × 3, 15 × 4, 12 × 5,
      10 × 6
   c) 1 × 100, 2 × 50, 4 × 25, 5 × 20, 10 × 10
4. 8, 56

Pages 38–39
Challenge 1
1. a) 230   b) 318   c) 248   d) 111
2. a) 216 (calculation set out as a column
     multiplication)
   b) 360 (calculation set out as a column
     multiplication)
   c) 672 (calculation set out as a column
     multiplication)
3. a) 4   b) 3
Challenge 2
1. a) 1518   b) 3035   c) 4459
2. a) 725 × 6 = 700 × **6** + 20 × **6** + 5 × **6**
      = 4350
   b) 2

3. a) 2989 (calculation set out as a column
     multiplication)
   b) 4098 (calculation set out as a column
     multiplication)
   c) 3843 (calculation set out as a column
     multiplication)
Challenge 3
1. a) 5992 (calculation set out as a column
     multiplication)
   b) 7736 (calculation set out as a column
     multiplication)
   c) 8604 (calculation set out as a column
     multiplication)
2. a) 547 × 7 = 3829   b) 385 × 9 = 3465
   c) 276 × 8 = 2208
3. 643 × 6 = 3858

Pages 40–41
Challenge 1
1. 288
2. 280
3. 60
4. £8.75
5. 168
Challenge 2
1. 744
2. 1536
3. £4170
4. 1390
5. 3800
Challenge 3
1. a) £2430   b) £2928   c) £2790
   d) £5176   e) £2422

Pages 42–45
Progress Test 1
1. a) 72, 78   b) 875, 900
2. 5274, 5427, 5472, 5724, 5742
3. a) <   b) <
4. £7799
5. a) 5835   b) 5008
6. 2390 circled
7. 8354
8. a) 38   b) 64
9. XLII circled
10. 535
11. a) 40
   b) Any number ≥184 but ≤186
12. a) 500   b) 800   c) 100

Answers

13.

	Rounded to the nearest 10 is	Rounded to the nearest 100 is	Rounded to the nearest 1000 is
5826	5830	5800	6000

14. −10, −20

15. −5

16. a) 240 **b)** 1080 **c)** 545

17. a) 527 − 353 = 174 **b)** 358 + 551 = 909

18. 372 + 322 circled

19. 282 (accept 365)

20. 599 minutes

21. 33 kilometres

22. a) 35 **b)** 27 **c)** 84
d) 8 **e)** 12 **f)** 6

23.

×	6	9	12
4	24	36	48
9	54	81	108
7	42	63	84

(1 mark for each correct row)

24. a) 75 **b)** 16 **c)** 88
d) 18 **e)** 12 **f)** 102

25. a) 1 and 20, 2 and 10, 4 and 5
b) 1 and 100, 2 and 50, 4 and 25, 5 and 20, 10 and 10

26. a) 378 **b)** 1060 **c)** 4256

27. 24

28. 54 × 3 = 50 × 3 + **4** × **3** = 162 (accept 4 and 3 in either order)

29. 35 metres

30. 100

Pages 46–47
Challenge 1

1. a) $\frac{3}{10}$ **b)** $\frac{9}{10}$ **c)** $\frac{7}{10}$

2. a) $\frac{9}{100}, \frac{13}{100}$ **b)** $\frac{79}{100}, \frac{80}{100}$ (accept $\frac{8}{10}$), $\frac{81}{100}$

3. 100

Challenge 2

1. a) $\frac{7}{100}$ **b)** $\frac{43}{100}$ **c)** $\frac{89}{100}$

2. a) $\frac{6}{100}$ (accept $\frac{3}{50}$) **b)** $\frac{9}{100}$

c) $\frac{2}{100}$ (accept $\frac{1}{50}$)

3. $\frac{1}{20}$ of a litre (accept $\frac{5}{100}$ or equivalent)

4. 1 cm

Challenge 3

1. $5 \div 100 = \frac{5}{100}$ circled

2. 1 ÷ 100 and 0.1 ÷ 10 circled

3. a) 7 **b)** 5 **c)** 0.7

4. a) 6 **b)** 10

Pages 48–49
Challenge 1

1. a) $\frac{3}{6} = \frac{1}{2}$ **b)** $\frac{4}{8} = \frac{1}{2}$

2. a) $\frac{5}{10}$ **b)** $\frac{6}{10}$ **c)** $\frac{8}{10}$

3. a) $\frac{4}{8}$ **b)** $\frac{2}{6}$ **c)** $\frac{3}{4}$

Challenge 2

1. a) $\frac{10}{20}$ **b)** $\frac{6}{20}$ **c)** $\frac{12}{20}$

2. a) $\frac{5}{15}$ **b)** $\frac{10}{15}$ **c)** $\frac{9}{15}$

3. a) $\frac{4}{12}, \frac{5}{15}, \frac{6}{18}, \frac{7}{21}, \frac{8}{24}$ **b)** $\frac{12}{16}, \frac{15}{20}, \frac{18}{24}, \frac{21}{28}, \frac{24}{32}$

Challenge 3

1. a) $\frac{10}{20}$ **b)** $\frac{16}{20}$ **c)** $\frac{6}{20}$
d) $\frac{1}{4}$ **e)** $\frac{2}{5}$ **f)** $\frac{9}{10}$

2. $\frac{8}{30}$ and $\frac{20}{100}$ circled

3. $\frac{2}{5}$

Pages 50–51
Challenge 1

1. a) $\frac{3}{5} + \frac{1}{5} = \frac{4}{5}$ **b)** $\frac{5}{6} - \frac{4}{6} = \frac{1}{6}$

2. a) $\frac{3}{3}$ or 1 **b)** $\frac{13}{8}$ or $1\frac{5}{8}$
c) $\frac{17}{10}$ or $1\frac{7}{10}$

3. a) $\frac{3}{5}$ **b)** $\frac{3}{10}$ **c)** $\frac{1}{8}$

Challenge 2

1. a) $\frac{4}{5} + \frac{2}{5} = \frac{6}{5} = 1\frac{1}{5}$
b) $\frac{4}{6} + \frac{4}{6} = \frac{8}{6} = 1\frac{2}{6}$ or $1\frac{1}{3}$

2. a) $\frac{4}{3} = 1\frac{1}{3}$ **b)** $\frac{7}{5} = 1\frac{2}{5}$
c) $\frac{6}{4} = 1\frac{2}{4}$ or $1\frac{1}{2}$

3. a) $\frac{3}{10}$ **b)** $\frac{5}{12}$ **c)** $\frac{9}{10}$

Challenge 3

1. a) $\frac{5}{5} - \frac{3}{5} = \frac{2}{5}$ (accept $1 - \frac{3}{5} = \frac{2}{5}$)
b) $\frac{3}{4} + \frac{3}{4} = \frac{6}{4}$ or $1\frac{2}{4}$ or $1\frac{1}{2}$

Answers

2. a) $\frac{5}{10}$ (accept $\frac{1}{2}$)   b) $\frac{6}{12}$ (accept $\frac{1}{2}$)
    c) $\frac{9}{8}$ (accept $1\frac{1}{8}$)

3. a) $\frac{5}{8}$ b) $\frac{6}{7}$ c) $\frac{3}{10}$

Pages 52–53
Challenge 1
1. a) 5   b) 6
    c) 6 m   d) 4 kg
2. a) 16   b) 16
    c) 27 ml   d) 25 km
3. 2 km
4. 14
Challenge 2
1. a) 7   b) 4
    c) £2   d) 2 m
2. a) 14   b) 28
    c) 55 cm   d) 6 km
3. 24 kg
4. 30
Challenge 3
1. a) 35   b) 45
2. 9
3. a) 20   b) 30
4. 15
5. Explanation that shows half of 27 is not a whole number or that $13\frac{1}{2}$ boys or girls cannot be possible.
6. a) 4   b) 20

Pages 54–55
Challenge 1
1. $\frac{3}{4}$ = 0.75, $\frac{1}{2}$ = 0.5, $\frac{1}{4}$ = 0.25
2. a) 0.1   b) 0.7   c) 0.3
3. a) 0.9   b) 1.6   c) 2.4   d) 5.5
4. a) 0.4   b) 0.8   c) 1
Challenge 2
1. a) 0.5   b) 0.25   c) 0.75
2. a) 0.9   b) 0.57   c) 0.03
3. £4.57
4. a) 0.3   b) 0.65   c) 0.95
Challenge 3
1. a) 0.09   b) 0.2   c) 1.01
2. a) 0.15
    b) Any number >0.45, <0.48
    c) Any number >0.8, <0.84
3. James is incorrect because 0.7 as a fraction is $\frac{7}{10}$, whereas $\frac{7}{100}$ is 0.07.
4. a) 10   b) 10

Pages 56–57
Challenge 1
1. a) 5   b) 5   c) 3
    d) 6   e) 8   f) 3
2. 3 m
3. 1 litre
4. Any number ≥6.5 but <7
Challenge 2
1. a) 7   b) 7   c) 22
    d) 54   e) 86   f) 105
2   50 kg
3. Any number ≥49.5 but <50.5
4. 29.7 and 30.4 circled
Challenge 3
1. a) 116   b) 230   c) 707
2. 100.3 and 99.6 circled
3. 13
4. 48.7 and 49.4 → 49
    49.8, 50.4 and 49.5 → 50

Pages 58–59
Challenge 1
1. 0.8 circled
2. 2.4 circled
3. 4.7, 5.6, 5.9, 6.2
4. Craig
5. Any number >7.6 but <8
Challenge 2
1. 12.16 circled
2. 34.45, 35.44, 43.54, 45.34, 45.43
3. 60.56
4. Any number >23.56 but <23.62
5. Any number >45.34 but <45.43 in the first space and any number >45.27 but <45.34 in the second space
Challenge 3
1. a) <   b) >
2. a) 3.76 m   b) 2.88 m
3.

4. 5.25, 6, 25.5, 50, 52.5

Pages 60–61
Challenge 1
1. a) 0.6   b) 1.2   c) 0.07
    d) 0.25
2. a) 5   b) 36   c) 6.3
3. a) 0.7 (accept seven tenths)
    b) 7 (accept seven ones)
    c) 0.07 (accept seven hundredths)
4. 0.25 kg

Challenge 2
1. a) 0.67   b) 0.54
   c) 0.15   d) 7.8
2. a) 5.7   b) 36
   c) 100   d) 100
3. 60
4. a) 0.04 (accept four hundredths)
   b) 0.04 (accept four hundredths)
5. £0.64 (accept 64p if £ sign is crossed out)

Challenge 3
1. a) 10   b) 100
   c) 32   d) 79
2. Many possible solutions:
   Kagendo's calculation, e.g. 9 ÷ 100 = 0.09
   Sally's calculation, e.g. 9 ÷ 10 = 0.9
3. 6.7 ÷ 10 and 56 ÷ 10 circled
4. a) 45 ÷ 10
   b) 60.8 ÷ 10

Pages 62–63
Challenge 1
1. a) £9.25   b) £5.05
   c) A set of pens and a book
2. 3 litres
3. 25 km
4. £2.40

Challenge 2
1. £5.11
2. £1.05
3. 1.35 kg
4. £8.10

Challenge 3
1. 12 kg
2. 10
3. a) 22.2 km   b) 20.8 km   c) 15.4 km

Pages 64–67
Progress Test 2
1. a) 77, 84
   b) 7000, 8000
2. 1384, 1834, 4138, 8314, 8341
3. 1 ten circled
4. a) and b) Accept any two different combinations of numbers that total 538, e.g. 300 + 200 + 38

5.

Number	Rounded to the nearest 10
3784	3780
427	430
79	80

6. −6

7. a) 6998   b) 4746
8. 600 + 400 = 1000
9. 318
10. 149 m
11. a) 72   b) 240
12. 168
13. a) 2128   b) 7520   c) 3768
14. 4 children share **6** paint pots and **10** brushes.
15. 48 × 3 = **40** x 3 + 8 × 3 = 144
16. a) $\frac{3}{100}$ (accept 0.03)
   b) $\frac{9}{100}$ (accept 0.09)
   c) $\frac{7}{100}$ (accept 0.07)
17. a) $\frac{7}{100}$ b) $\frac{16}{100}$
18. a) $\frac{3}{4}$ b) $\frac{5}{10}$
19. a) $\frac{11}{10}$ or $1\frac{1}{10}$ b) $\frac{9}{8}$ or $1\frac{1}{8}$
20. a) $\frac{13}{100}$ b) $\frac{9}{10}$ (accept $\frac{90}{100}$)   c) $\frac{9}{100}$
21. a) 0.93   b) 0.07   c) 0.4
22. a) 5   b) 15   c) 30
23. Accept any of the following: 24.5, 24.6, 24.7, 24.8, 24.9
24. 73.8 circled
25. 30.2, 30.7, 31.6, 31.8, 32.5
26. a) 10   b) 100   c) 100   d) 10
27. 57
28. a) 10   b) 24   c) 81
29. £29 (accept £29.00; do not accept £29.0)

Pages 68–69
Challenge 1
1. 83.76 m, 83.67 m, 63.78 m, 38.76 m, 36.87 m
2. 4.87 litres, 5.47 litres, 45.78 litres, 54.87 litres, 78.54 litres
3. Accept any capacity >4.56 litres but <4.75 litres
4. 1.25 m, $1\frac{1}{2}$ m, 1.65 m
5. Dubry

Challenge 2
1. a) 3.2 kg circled   b) 8000 g circled
2. a) 474 cm circled   b) 6 cm circled
3. a) 5.675 litres circled   b) 10 litres circled
4. 4.7 m, 475 cm, 4800 mm, 5 m
5. No

Challenge 3
1. 4.8 m circled
2. 4500 metres circled
3. 1 litre bottle circled
4. B, C, A

Answers

Pages 70–71
Challenge 1
1. Accept any mass >3.5 kg but <3.9 kg
2. Accept any length >7.4 cm but <7.8 cm
3. 0.75 litre
4. £24.75 and £26.15 ticked
Challenge 2
1. 4 m ticked
2. 350 ml ticked
3. 120 g ticked
4. 12 minutes ticked
Challenge 3
1. £15
2. Accept any temperature >26°C but <30°C
3. Accept any length >7 cm but <10 cm
4. Accept any mass >2 kg but <2.5 kg

Pages 72–73
Challenge 1
1. a) 3 cm   b) 4 m   c) 5 km
   d) 60 mm   e) 500 cm   f) 9000 m
   g) 4 kg   h) 40 kg   i) 5000 g
   j) 8000 ml k) 10 litres l) 500 ml
2. 4
3. a) Yes   b) 5 cm or 50 mm
Challenge 2
1. a) 520 cm   b) 3500 g   c) 3.5 litres
   d) 7.8 cm   e) 0.25 km   f) 75 cm
   g) 8.45 m   h) 10.5 km
2. 400 g or 0.4 kg
3. Jug B
4. 68 ml
Challenge 3
1. 1000 mm
2. a) m   b) cm   c) km
   d) litres   e) g   f) cm
3.

| $\frac{1}{2}$ litre | 300 ml | 200 ml |

| 0.6 litres |

| $\frac{1}{4}$ litre | 200 ml | 550 ml |

(accept equivalent measures, e.g. $\frac{1}{5}$ litre)

Pages 74–75
Challenge 1
1. £1.55
2. £13.24
3. £4 (accept £4.00; do not accept £4.0)
4. £4.95
5. £2.67

Challenge 2
1. a) £7.10   b) 3.76 m
   c) 18.20 kg   d) 46.79 litres
2. £36.60
3. 6.5 kg
4. 9.25 m
5. 15 litres
Challenge 3
1. a) 3.55 kg   b) 3550 g
2. 50p
3. Accept three 0.6 m cupboards and three 0.4 m cupboards or six 0.4 m cupboards and one 0.6 m cupboard.
4. 4

Pages 76–77
Challenge 1
1. a) 4:10am   b) 7:25am   c) 4:55am
2. a) 18:45   b) 17:05   c) 21:35
3. a) Twenty past eight or 20 past 8
   b) Five past eight or 5 past 8
   c) Twenty to eleven or 20 to 11
Challenge 2
1. a) 3:25pm   b) 6:10pm
2. a) 14:15   b) 11:50   c) 18:35
3. 12:15 or quarter past 12 or $\frac{1}{4}$ past 12 or 00:15
Challenge 3
1.

	Word time		12 hour time		24 hour time
a)	Five past two in the afternoon	=	2:05pm	=	14:05
b)	Twenty-five to 9 in the evening	=	8:35pm	=	20:35

2. 40 minutes

Pages 78–79
Challenge 1
1. a) 120 seconds   b) 120 minutes
   c) 48 hours   d) 14 days
2. April, June, September and November
3. 2024
4. 8th May
Challenge 2
1. Accept 2 hours 20 minutes or 140 minutes
2. 40 minutes
3. Accept 19:15, 7:15, 7:15pm or quarter past 7
4. a) 28 days   b) 24 months
   c) 300 seconds   d) 72 hours
Challenge 3
1. Accept any time >8 minutes but <10 minutes
2. a) 336 hours = 14 days = 2 weeks
   b) 120 months = 10 years = 1 decade
3. Accept 06:45, 6:45, 6:45am or quarter to 7

4. 3 hours 5 minutes
5. Accept 13:27, 1:27, 1:27pm **or** 27 past 1

Pages 80–81
Challenge 1
1. A a) 8 squares   b) 12 cm
   B a) 9 squares   b) 12 cm
   C a) 10 squares   b) 22 cm
Challenge 2
1. A a) 9 squares   b) 16 cm
   B a) 16 squares   b) 20 cm
   C a) 7 squares   b) 16 cm
2. 28 cm
Challenge 3
1. a) 2 cm   b) 5 small squares
2. 14 cm

Pages 82–85
Progress Test 3
1. a) 63, 72, 81, **90**, 99, 108
   b) 36, **42**, **48**, 54, 60, 66
2. 3752, 3727, 3725, 3572, 3527
3. 6548
4. LXV circled
5.

Number	Rounded to the nearest hundred
7 8 2 3	7800
7 8 2	800
7 8	100

6. a) 545   b) 502
7. a) 6   b) 6
   c) 5   d) 49
8. 8
9. a) 4581   b) 3164   c) 5166
10. 6 hours
11. a) 100   b) 10   c) 10
12. A line drawn from $\frac{3}{5}$ to $\frac{6}{10}$
13. a) $\frac{1}{8}$ b) $\frac{3}{12}$
14. £19
15. £10
16. a) Balloons, candles and a cake
    b) £2.55
17. £3, £1.25, 90p, £0.08, 5p
18. a) Tia   b) Raf
19. £40
20. 15 minutes
21. Clock **B** circled
22. Statement **A** ticked
23. 1 minute 40 seconds

24. a) 5000 g   b) 6 cm   c) 10 m
    d) 8 litres   e) 800 cm   f) 2000 m
25. a) 13 cm   b) 12 cm
26. 25 squares

Pages 86–87
Challenge 1
1. Shapes **A** and **C** ticked
2. a) B and D   b) A and D
   c) C   d) B
3. Shape **B** ticked
Challenge 2
1. Shapes **B** and **D** ticked
2. A hexagon has six sides. This is a pentagon as it has five sides.
3. Triangle **B** ticked
Challenge 3
1. Octagon circled
2. Shapes **A**, **B** and **C** ticked
3. Any pentagon drawn with a right angle.

Pages 88–89
Challenge 1
1. Shape **A** ticked
2. Shape **C** ticked
3. a) 6   b) 6
Challenge 2
1. a) 7   b) 4
2. Statement **D** ticked
3.

Shape	Faces	Edges	Vertices
Cuboid	6	12	8
Square-based pyramid	5	8	5
Triangular prism	5	9	6

(1 mark for each correct row)
Challenge 3
1. Yes, Shona is correct. On each face, the angles at the vertices are right angles and the opposite edges are equal and parallel. These are the properties of a rectangle.
2. Pentagon
3. a) 5   b) 7

Pages 90–91
Challenge 1
1.

Answers

2.

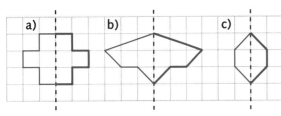

Challenge 2

1. a) 4   **b)** 2   **c)** 2

2.

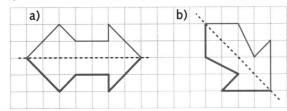

Challenge 3

1. Shape **D** ticked
2. Different answers are possible, e.g.:

or

Pages 92–93
Challenge 1

1. a) 4   **b)** 6   **c)** 4
2. Angle **B** ticked
3. Angle **A** ticked
4. Angle **D** ticked

Challenge 2

1.

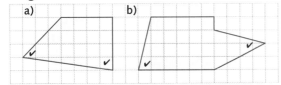

2. B, D, A, C
3. obtuse, right, acute

Challenge 3

1. a) Any five-sided shape with three obtuse angles drawn, e.g.

b) Any four-sided shape with three acute angles drawn, e.g.

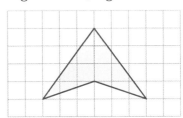

2. No, Caroline isn't correct. Triangles cannot have two right angles.

Pages 94–95
Challenge 1

1. a) C   **b)** D   **c)** F
    d) A   **e)** B
    f) Square **B** to square **D**

Challenge 2

1. a) 11 right, 1 down   **b)** 3 left, 3 up
    c) 7 left, 1 down   **d)** 11 right, 4 up
    e) 4 right, 2 down   **f)** 4 left, 3 down

Challenge 3

1. 5 (units) right, 7 (units) up
2.

3. a) row circled   **b)** column circled

Pages 96–97
Challenge 1

1. a) (4,6)   **b)** (2,7)   **c)** (6,4)
    d) (5,3)   **e)** (7,2)   **f)** (3,5)
2. a) Points (1,2) and (7,8) plotted and joined with a straight line.
    b) (4,5)

Challenge 2

1. a) A plotted at (6,1)   **b)** B plotted at (5,7)
    c) C plotted at (2,6)   **d)** D plotted at (7,4)
    e) E plotted at (1,3)   **f)** F plotted at (4,2)

2. **a)** (5,3)   **b)** (5,3)

Challenge 3
1. **a)** (6,3) written and plotted on the grid
    b) (7,3) written and plotted on the grid
    c) (2,4) written and plotted on the grid
    d) (7,6) written and plotted on the grid
    (1 mark for each pair of coordinates written correctly; 1 mark for each pair of coordinates plotted correctly)

Pages 98–99
Challenge 1
1. **a) and b)** Rectangle plotted with vertices at (1,7), (1,4), (6,7) and (6,4)
    c) (6,4)
2. **a)** (7,3) and (3,1) plotted
    b) A right-angled triangle drawn
    c) The third vertex could be: (0,7), (1,5), (2,3), (3,3), (4,4), (5,7), (6,0), (6,5), (7,1) **or** (8,1)

Challenge 2
1. **a) and b)** Square plotted with vertices at (3,8), (1,6), (5,6) and (3,4)
    c) (3,4)
2. **a) and b)** Kite plotted with vertices at (6,6), (4,4), (8,4) and (6,3) **or** (6,6), (4,4), (8,4) and (6,2) **or** (6,6), (4,4), (8,4) and (6,1) **or** (6,6), (4,4), (8,4) and (6,0)
    c) (6,3) **or** (6,2) **or** (6,1) **or** (6,0)

Challenge 3
1. (15,10)
2. (9,9) (accept (–1,4))
3. **a)** (5,5)   **b)** (5,5)
4. No, Daria is not correct. The *x*-axis displays lines that are vertical. If they are all the same the line would be vertical.

Pages 100–101
Challenge 1
1. **a)** 2   **b)** Red   **c)** Orange
    d) Blue   **e)** 15

Challenge 2
1. **a)** 3   **b)** 38 circled   **c)** 42
    d) 4   **e)** 4

Challenge 3
1. **a)** 19   **b)** 196
    c) 2 second places = 10 points
    4 third places = 8 points
    or
    9 third places = 18 points
    d) Yes, Simon could be correct. Many possible explanations, e.g. 10 second places = 50 points.

Pages 102–103
Challenge 1
1. **a)** 9:00am   **b)** 8°C   **c)** 6°C
    d) 7 hours
    e) 3

Challenge 2
1. **a)** 12:00   **b)** 5 hours
    c) 1 hour
    d) 5°C
    e) Any time between 10:20 and 10:40

Challenge 3
1. **a)** 1°C
    b) 6°C
    c) Any temperature >4°C but <5°C
    d) Any time between 3 hours 30 minutes and 3 hours 45 minutes
    e) Any time between 1 hour 35 minutes and 1 hour 50 minutes

Pages 104–105
Challenge 1
1. **a)** 4   **b)** 28   **c)** 12
    d) 8   **e)** 5

Challenge 2
1. **a)** Sami and Ava   **b)** 100 km
    c) 40 km   **d)** 3

Challenge 3
1. **a)** 60   **b)** 100
    c) 40   **d)** 120

Pages 106–107
Challenge 1
1. **a)** £18   **b)** £32   **c)** £7   **d)** £13

Challenge 2
1. **a)** 5
    b) Hot meal total = 47, added to table
    c) Class A children who had a sandwich = 5, added to table
    d) Class C children who had a vegetarian meal = 9, added to table

Challenge 3
1. **a)** 38
    b) Yes, Olivia is correct. The Friday column shows 24 men visiting. Saturday (18) and Sunday (6) total 24.
    c) 5
    d) Women (accept 76)

Pages 108–111
Progress Test 4
1. 9018, 9108, 9180, 9801, 9810
2. **a)** four hundreds **or** 400
    b) four thousands **or** 4000
    c) four tens **or** 40

Answers

3. 56
4. **a)** 7503 + **18**12 = 9315
    b) **854** − **3**62 = 492
5. 146
6. $\frac{5}{12}$
7. 2 kg
8. 4100 g, $4\frac{1}{2}$ kg, 4.9 kg, 5 kg, 5500 g
9. 21
10. **a)** 19:35   **b)** 20:45   **c)** 18:50
    (1 mark for all three parts correct)
11. **a)** 8 kg   **b)** 9000 ml
    c) 50 cm   **d)** 450 cm
12. 8.25 litres
13. **a)** 4.5 kg **or** 4500 g
    b) 4.5 m **or** 450 cm

14. right-angled and scalene circled
15. **a)** 2   **b)** 0
16. Obtuse
17. The square has moved **3** squares to the left and **1** square up.
18. **a)** A
    b) Accept any of the following coordinates:
    (1,8), (2,7), (7,2), (8,1)
19. **a)** 155   **b)** 137   **c)** 15
20. **a)** 7 mm
    b) Tuesday and Wednesday
    c) 2
21. **a)** Kay   **b)** 8

Notes

Progress Test Charts

Progress Test 1

Q	Topic	✓ or ✗	See page
1	Counting		12
2	Numbers Beyond 1000		14
3	Numbers Beyond 1000		14
4	Numbers Beyond 1000		14
5	Numbers Beyond 1000		14
6	Place Value		16
7	Place Value		16
8	Roman Numerals		18
9	Roman Numerals		18
10	Representing Numbers		20
11	Representing Numbers		20
12	Rounding Numbers		22
13	Rounding Numbers		22
14	Negative Numbers		24
15	Negative Numbers		24
16	Addition and Subtraction Practice		26
17	Addition and Subtraction Practice		26
18	Estimating and Checking Calculations		28
19	Estimating and Checking Calculations		28
20	Addition and Subtraction Problems		30
21	Addition and Subtraction Problems		30
22	Multiplication and Division Facts		32
23	Multiplication and Division Facts		32
24	Factors		36
25	Factors		36
26	Multiplication Practice		38
27	Multiplication Problems		40
28	Multiplication Problems		40
29	Multiplication Problems		40
30	Multiplication Problems		40

Progress Test 2

Q	Topic	✓ or ✗	See page
1	Counting		12
2	Numbers Beyond 1000		14
3	Place Value		16
4	Representing Numbers		20
5	Rounding Numbers		22
6	Negative Numbers		24
7	Addition and Subtraction Practice		26
8	Estimating and Checking Calculations		28
9	Addition and Subtraction Problems		30
10	Addition and Subtraction Problems		30
11	Factors		36
12	Factors		36
13	Multiplication Practice		38
14	Multiplication Problems		40
15	Multiplication Problems		40
16	Hundredths		46
17	Hundredths		46
18	Equivalent Fractions		48
19	Addition and Subtraction of Fractions		50
20	Fraction and Decimal Equivalents		54
21	Fraction and Decimal Equivalents		54
22	Rounding Decimals		56
23	Rounding Decimals		56
24	Comparing Decimals		58
25	Comparing Decimals		58
26	Dividing by 10 and 100		60
27	Dividing by 10 and 100		60
28	Finding Fractions		52
29	Decimal Problems		62

Progress Test Charts

Progress Test 3

Q	Topic	✓ or ✗	See page
1	Counting		12
2	Numbers Beyond 1000		14
3	Place Value		16
4	Roman Numerals		18
5	Rounding Numbers		22
6	Addition and Subtraction Problems		30
7	Multiplication and Division Facts		32
8	Factors		36
9	Multiplication Practice		38
10	Multiplication Problems		40
11	Hundredths		46
12	Equivalent Fractions		48
13	Addition and Subtraction of Fractions		50
14	Rounding Decimals		56
15	Finding Fractions		52
16	Decimal Problems		62
17	Comparing Measures		68
18	Comparing Measures		68
19	Estimating Measures		70
20	12 and 24 Hour Time		76
21	12 and 24 Hour Time		76
22	Time Problems		78
23	Time Problems		78
24	Converting Measures		72
25	Perimeter and Area		80
26	Perimeter and Area		80

Progress Test 4

Q	Topic	✓ or ✗	See page
1	Numbers Beyond 1000		14
2	Place Value		16
3	Representing Numbers		20
4	Addition and Subtraction Practice		26
5	Multiplication Problems		40
6	Addition and Subtraction of Fractions		50
7	Finding Fractions		52
8	Comparing Measures		68
9	Time Problems		78
10	12 and 24 Hour Time		76
11	Converting Measures		72
12	Measurement Calculations		74
13	Measurement Calculations		74
14	2-D Shapes		86
15	Lines of Symmetry		90
16	Angles		92
17	Translations		94
18	Coordinates / Shapes and Coordinates		96 / 98
19	Tables		106
20	Time Graphs		102
21	Bar Charts		100

What am I doing well in? _____

_____

What do I need to improve? _____

_____